ON THE JOURNEY OF JUST BEING

Finding Yourself on the Greatest Paths of Purpose

L. GARDENHIRE

Copyright © 2018 L. Gardenhire
All rights reserved. No part of this book may be reproduced, distributed, or transmitted in any form or by any electronic or mechanical means, including information storage and retrieval systems, without written permission from the publisher, except in the case of brief quotations embodied in critical reviews and certain other noncommercial uses permitted by copyright law. For permission requests, write to the publisher, addressed "Attention: Permissions," at the address below.

ISBN 978-1-7338382-0-7
Library of Congress Control Number 2019903029

Printed in the United States of America
First Printed in 2019

Although the author and publisher have made every effort to ensure that the information in this book was correct at press time, the author and publisher do not assume and hereby disclaim any liability to any party for any loss, damage, or disruption caused by errors or omissions, whether such errors or omissions result from negligence, accident, or any other cause. This book is not intended as a substitute for the medical advice of physicians or mental health professionals. The reader should regularly consult a physician and/or other health care providers in matters relating to his/her health, and particularly with respect to any symptoms that may require diagnosis or medical attention.

Edited by Glow and Mary

Published by Lagan Gate, LLC
PO Box 11017
Riviera Beach, FL 33419
Visit us at *www.LaganGate.com*

To Dorothy,
May your spirit always fill the sole of my shoes
May your love forever guide the paths of my walk
To exude the greatness, you graciously bestow to us

Table of Contents

1. What Does It Mean to Be? 11

Introduction   11
To Be...   13
The Basis of Being   18
The Evolution of Our Conformity   21

2. The Journey to Being 27

The 3 Fundamental Questions of Being   27
The 3 External Navigational Cues   30
The Repetition of Poor Results   32
The Hardship or Pleasure of Perception   36
Mastering the Journey of Being   37

3. Erasing the Ego 55

The Three Major Lies of the Ego   55
The Cycle of Confidence, Ego, and Humility   58
The Differences Between Ego and Esteem   61
Building Confidence Apart from Ego   64

4. The Development of the True Self 69

The Crossings of Comparison   69
The Faults of Competition   75
Literally, Minding Our Own Businesses   77
The Illusory Reward of Self-Falsehood   83
The New Technological You   86
The Four Main Routes of Personal Escapism   87

5 Your Power as One 97

Honoring Our Power as One 97
The Forgiveness of The Past Self 101
The Acceptance of The Present Self 103
The Preparation for the Future Self 106
The Silent Treatment 109
Meditation 111
Prayer 113
Relaxation 114
Re-Aligning with Nature 116

6 The Bold Act of Being Still 119

Fight nor Flight 119
Fighting Life 121
Rest 127
Unplug and Declutter 132

7 Being in Relationships 141

The Mirroring of Beings 141
The Devaluation of Bad Relationships 144
Revenge, Resentment, and the Natural Law of
 Received Emotions 149

8 Being Spiritual 157

Reaching Your Greatest Self 157
Why Spirituality is Key 159
Unlocking the God in You 161
You Are Enough 164
Obtaining a Piece of Peace, Happiness, and Love 171

9 Being of Purpose 181

    The Purpose of our Purposes   181
    The Equations of Purpose   184
    The Proponents of Doing   188
    Being Guided into Our Purposes   191
    You Already Matter   194
    You Are Already Different   195

10 Growing Your Greatest You 201

    Mastering the Art of Transitions   201
    The Conscious Be'er   206
    Teaching the Power of Self   212
    The Conclusion to the Continuation of Just Being   215

On the Journey *of Just* *Being...*

SECTION 1
of Position
(in Time & Space)

tween **Bey**ond **Beh**in
ong **Be***side* **Be**fore **Be**
elated **Be**neath **Be**lo

CHAPTER 1
What Does It Mean to Be?

> *"We often solely aim to be, practice to be, learn to be, seek permission to be, and want, hope, and wish to be, when most times, on the journey of just being, we accomplish just that, and we are aptly able to just be."*

INTRODUCTION

I came across the term *"Just Be"* oddly enough from a song made popular on the internet. From the moment I heard it, the words captured my attention, and the phrase began to resonate from within. For such a simple saying, it became a massive window of introspection, allowing me to profoundly see my ideas, actions, and behaviors, and have them revolve around the short term as sync and as appropriate as the planets around the sun. And well, for obvious reasons, it instantly became one of my favorites.

Soon enough, as fate would have it, I began to adopt these two words as my personal motto. I began to personally and spiritually expound on

ON THE JOURNEY OF JUST BEING

just what it meant to *"just be."* Little did I know that it would be these two words that would aid in the creation of this book and, ultimately, the rediscovering of my own enduring truth.

Just like all of us at some point in our lives, I sensed that I had begun to lose myself. My center had shifted, and my balance became everything but. At the time, I felt foreign to my being, distant from myself even though I had been bound to my physicality and enveloped tightly in my own wrapping and securing skin. But in all that I lost, I did gain measures unimaginable because what I found was nothing short of destiny, as who I found was *me*.

As I made my way back to personal authenticity, I took a host of mental notes until this book, true to *"just being"*, manifested itself to fruition.

As an acting guide for me, it is my sincerest hope that readers find the same or greater use of this reading, such that they are propelled into a richness of being, spreading such innovation, love, and purpose as far out as the universe is wide.

For I, and perhaps you, have experienced that it is just being that takes us out of a state of want and places us directly into a state of I am. And instead of waiting to be on a particular path, when we are engaged in being, we are instantly positioned upon the path of our desired journey.

With that said, we often solely aim to be, practice to be, learn to be, seek permission to be, and want, hope, and wish to be, when most times, on the journey of just being, we accomplish just that, and we are aptly

What Does It Mean to Be?

able to *just be*.

Being is how we find ourselves, it is how we find the world, and it is how we find ourselves in what can be an overwhelming and sometimes unforgiving world. But most importantly, it is how we find the world in ourselves. Because being shows us all what we can become when we choose to manifest naturally all that we truly are, and for that reason alone should it, should we, be treasured.

We don't need to ask to be what we are already are. This is because even though we are humans, we are always more, as we are human beings. Yes, that's right, human *"be-ings."*

And that is why as beings we must do what beings do, naturally, and in our most authentic form, we must, well, be.

But before we go further on this journey of just being, it will help to first fundamentally understand what exactly it means to be?

TO BE…

In this life of purpose and personal awareness, we all, in many areas and points of our lives, strive to be somebody. But without the will and knowing how to successfully *be*, many of us are left only to

> **"**
> Without the will and knowing how to successfully **BE**, many of us are left only to exist as **SOMEBODY**, only left to hold and embody the dull essence of some body.

ON THE JOURNEY OF JUST BEING

exist as somebody, only left to hold and embody the dull essence of *some* body.

You see, it is being that welds our identity to truth and adds meaning to our lives. It is the core of us that makes all the difference, and that is why it is so significant.

To be is essentially finding and becoming the best you, and then using yourself in the greatest capacity, and ironically, with the greatest of ease. To be is to be authentic, it is to be purposeful, and it is, in many aspects, to be largely certain of who you are. Overall, it is to live, to live the life you've always wanted, to do more than just follow your dreams, but to reside in them, to just *be* them. If one wants to be a singer, they must be of song and sing. If one wants to be a writer, they must be of words and write. And if one wants to actively engage in being, they must authentically learn the varied practices and mechanisms of just being.

Being doesn't have to be a complicated process. But like all things worthwhile, it does and will require work. Fortunately for us, being requires a lot less work than the alternative, and from its presence, we become all or more than we could ever imagine.

So, what exactly do we get from being? Well, the prefix *"Be-"* gives us a better understanding of what it means to essentially be.

1. To Be is Position (in both space and time):

Belong: Rightfully positioned among persons or objects

What Does It Mean to Be?

> Between: Positioned in the space separating persons or objects
>
> Belated: Positioned afterward
>
> Beyond: Positioned further

To be is to know the position of ourselves in relation to the world outside and inside of us. By positioning ourselves on the right paths, we can find and explore our authentic selves, and more importantly, we begin to understand just how to appropriately put such a being to greater use.

Our positions should often be on the journeys and paths that take us to a place of authenticity and of just being. It is the place where the seed not only recognizes that it is a seed, but also, where and when to appropriately take root.

2. **To Be is Creation:**

> Become: In the process of creating something or someone new
>
> Becharm: To create and possibly control prolonged attractions
>
> Begotten: Having been created
>
> Begin: To create a starting

Once you find your authentic self, you will certainly feel like someone new. That's why to be is creation. No, you won't be creating a new you altogether, but when engaged in being, we tend to create new courses and new and better beings, as we acknowledge and take part in new levels of authenticity and awareness.

ON THE JOURNEY OF JUST BEING

Just as a seed grows, creation gives us the consistency of still being, but also many opportunities for growth. New roots spread out as they begin to make space for our new becoming, acting as a pillar to support the advances for our maturation. You see, to be is not to create a whole new being in the physical sense, but rather to create portions of growth as we begin to embody all our true essences, all that is our greatest and most cherished sense of self.

3. **To Be is Greatness:**

   Bedazzle: To greatly impress

   Belaud: To greatly praise

   Beloved: To love someone greatly

4. **To Be is Causation/Influence:**

   Bethink: To cause thoughts or reminders

   Behalf: To be influenced by another in action and/or thoughts

When we are engaged in being on a higher level, our destiny and purpose allow us to foster betterment and influence positivity, ultimately leading us into a unique and personalized space of greatness.

To be great and of positive influence is the seed becoming so mighty that it can now rear seeds of its own, it can now feel an intense and undeniable awareness of self, as it is able to give real purpose, beauty, and life, even when life brings upon it struggles.

As you have now seen, the word *"be"* is inundated in the English

What Does It Mean to Be?

language so much that most of us don't even bother to pay attention to it. But there is one man in particular who has made this tiny word into a literary giant. He understood the importance of it and so seemingly had everyone else after writer and playwright, William Shakespeare masterfully orchestrated the phrase *"to be or not to be..."*

Since then, we have made and further popularized a host of words and phrases that attempt to subconsciously (or otherwise) facilitate a deeper connection to our beings and to our true selves. We so routinely say ourselves and myself that we hardly ever, if at any time, see the words for what they really are—*our selves, my self*.

When we are up to the journey of life, we aim to have high self-esteem, sharp self-awareness, and we hope to achieve the personal and possibly public accolades of self-actualization, as we reach and actually fulfill some of our highest potentials. You see, in order to establish and multiply our well-being, we must be willing to participate in, well, being.

In contrast, when our beings are not their true selves, we mundanely and nonchalantly say things like *"I haven't really been feeling like 'my self'"*, or *"I need to gather or get 'my self' together"*, not to mention *"I really wish you/they would just let me be!"*

So ask yourself, have you literally been your self? Do you even know what your self looks or feels like? Whatever your response may be, being is how we acknowledge and use the self to find, maintain, and produce the greatest version of our most authentic beings.

Because while the self is finite, our beings are infinite. And while the self is just a body, it is being that embodies all we know as good. It is spiritual, it is undying and unimaginably powerful. Just think even as you sit or stand, even in stillness and sometimes more so when you are being still, you have the ability to nurture and develop the power to not only better yourself but the world around you too. For what lies in your being is a surplus of potential, you being is just the practice of pulling all such potential out.

And while the self is a noun, the word *"be"*, for all of us, acts as both a noun and a verb. It is the self in purposeful motion. It is the self thriving with such intent, as we become the person, the place, and the thing all wrapped up in one invincible movement.

But before we delve more into the many ways to be, how to master it, and what will make it work for you, we must first learn how to acknowledge the fundamental characteristics of being and, sometimes, more importantly, the characteristics of not being. And in doing so, we must first discuss and further clarify a few simple terms.

THE BASIS OF BEING

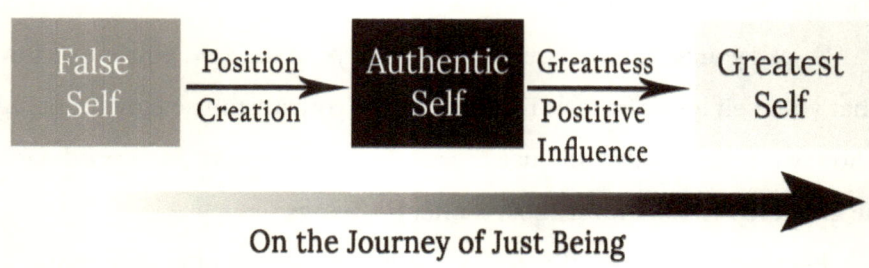

On the Journey of Just Being

What Does It Mean to Be?

The first term is the *False Self*. The false you, as the term implies, is the collective false personas of you. It is the ego, the need for power, and the constant need for insignificant validation. The false you is the person one might pretend to be. It is a compilation of all the identities others might impose on you, the mask people often wear to hide who they really are.

It is the feeling of hopelessness. It is the displeasure of one's self and the self eagerly and mistakenly wanting to be another. The false you is the sensation of being completely lost in the world around you, the sense of incompleteness, and the feeling of unworthiness, of not being rich from within.

The false you in one sentence is the direct result of not just being. It is the seed not realizing that it is, in fact, a seed. But there is hope.

The *Authentic Self* is the next step to being, and it occurs when you do just that, when one can just be. It is your authentic self that establishes and grows a rich identity, one that strongly aligns who you really are, who you are to be, and the journey and paths in life that connect them.

It is the seed grounded in its own truth. It is the seed being planted.

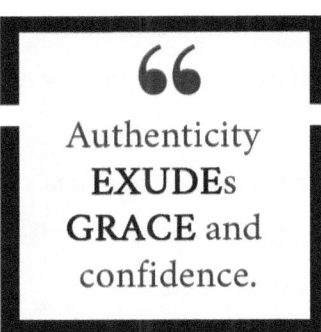

Authenticity exudes grace and confidence. And in all the ways the false being is false, our authentic beings are just the opposite. With that said, our authentic beings may not always be what we expect,

ON THE JOURNEY OF JUST BEING

as it practices candor alongside an acute sense of self-awareness. And unlike the conventional definition of self-consciousness, it acknowledges both the good and bad factors of our beings while encouraging the work needed to maintain and improve them. Our authentic selves do not scold, and they do not self-shame; they only seek to push us toward that of our greatest being, which brings us to the last term.

The *Greatest Self* is, of course, us at our greatest. This does not necessarily mean we are the greatest in the world, or the richest or most famous, but that we are our greatest version of our beings in a given period of time.

The greatest self is a mixture of one's mind, body, and soul at their highest capacities. It often acts independently from other beings, time, and the measure of one's situations, as it only corresponds to the condition of one's intellect, awareness, purpose, emotional stability, and the knowledge to be as best as one can at any particular moment.

For example, your greatest self at twenty years old won't be identical to your greatest self when you are fifty-five years old, or at any other age for that matter. That doesn't mean you will be more or less great; it just means that your greatest self has changed into a different and, hopefully, evolved module of being.

And this is a good thing, as it ensures that we can reach our greatest selves repeatedly in any moment after we've appropriately learned to perceive its many appearances. As it is our greatest selves that boldly realize we are no longer just a seed, that we now bare the decadent

What Does It Mean to Be?

flowers and the sweetest fruits of life, that we now can produce powerful seeds of our own.

It is our greatest self that is closest to our authenticity. It knows the benefits of good conformity but still holds true to its identity. It is the mighty tree being a mighty tree, but acknowledging, accepting, and loving the fact that its roots will spread about the earth different than others, that its limbs will twist a different dance in the breeze, and its leaves will be painted of varied style and beauty, even when they are blemished, and so too when they have fallen.

And as momentous as our sense of being is, so many of us fail to consistently reach the arc of our greatest self. Many of us are plainly choosing not to be as we decide to embody everything but the soul of who we really are. We hide behind smugness and stagnation, and we use the evolution of conformity to gift us a comforted complacency.

In fact, it is the evolution of conformity that leads a lot of us into a false state of being. That's why in order to initiate and endure our journey of just being we must understand just how it affects us and when and how to overcome it.

THE EVOLUTION OF OUR CONFORMITY

Obtaining an authentic state of being, for the most part, is a challenge that everyone has at some point in their lives. This is mostly due to the evolution of our conformity. When we look at the grand scheme of things, it seems as if we are instinctively apt to converge, and

ON THE JOURNEY OF JUST BEING

indeed we are.

The answer to our conformity lies in the past, and like most cultural and subconscious habits, it is linked to both our survival and evolutionary histories. The same reason a group of ancient men hunted mammoth together can be equated to explain why many high schoolers congregate in factions, and why countries fight to keep their boundaries marked and protected.

You see, there can be power, distinction, and a sense of togetherness in aggregations, and wherever such powers lie, safety, for the most part, is somewhere close. Safety brings us comfort and because of that, the ease, reassurance, and the convenience of our clustering is more easily passed on to following generations. After all, you really think those that hunted mammoth alone or in fewer numbers lived past the experience to pass on their genetic inheritance?

In our own lifetime, from the time we make our homes in the womb, we begin connecting to the world around us, as we listen and become familiar with the sounds of our parents' voices. When we are born, gender roles begin to pour on us. And in some ways, our parents begin to subconsciously or blatantly pour their ideologies, habits, and unfulfilled dreams, however good or bad, onto us.

By the time we are around two years of age and entering the autonomous stage, the *"let me," "I can do it myself"* phase of our lives, we willingly pick up whatever is thrown our way. It is there, I believe, that we first begin to consciously look at the world around us and

What Does It Mean to Be?

mold ourselves to its liking. Around five years of age, we continue this cycle as we begin to understand and experience both the benefits and horrors of social pressure from that of our peers and of society. Here, our confidence is not necessarily most gained by being who we truly are but by making those around us proud through, for example, athleticism, academics, fashion, and temperament.

By the time we reach high school, peer pressure is at its height. And instead of being ourselves, in the name of popularity and hormones, many of us pick up habits and partake in behaviors that will undoubtedly create and cling portions of falseness to our beings for at least some amount of time.

As our adolescences come to an end, larger bits and pieces of ourselves begin to show themselves. And though we begin to truly resurface in the discovering of our beings, within this day and age of technology and the virtual presence of everyone else, even at this stage in life, the act of just being is arguably becoming more overly complicated than it has ever been before. And still afterward, people in some instances find ways to harmfully come together or subconsciously conform to unnecessary guidelines.

We wear clothes that are trendy due in part to *"everyone else."* We buy products (sometimes solely) because they were endorsed by someone else. We allow our measures of success and self-worth to be determined by everyone else. Even though many have a voice in our political systems, a lot of decisions and laws are made in part by everyone else. We tune in and watch shows just because everyone else is watching them, and we often make decisions based off everyone's opinions and perceptions.

With that being said, there are some pros to *"everyone else,"* particularly those close to us. Culture is passed down through them, and so is food and dance and music. Language is spoken so much that we often pick it up before we realize we have. Morals and good behaviors too can be taught and relayed. And while these are great, we still need the individual and, even better, the individual at its highest potential, and here's why.

For progression to take place, we need the minds of those who can think and create differently and of those willing to encourage others to do the same. At times, being ourselves is not easy, especially when it unnecessarily and non-harmfully goes against *"everyone else's"* ideals. But the only progress that can be found in extreme conformity is the thought of breaking away from it, as it does no good for everyone to be too similar.

If all are swordsmen, we all would need blacksmiths, and if all are blacksmiths, we all would need miners. You see, we need variety in our populations so that it may benefit all of us in the greatest ways and

> " For PROGRESSion to take place, we need the minds of those who can think and create DIFFERENTLY.

What Does It Mean to Be?

make it easier to be ourselves as pressures within the realms of extreme conformity are excessively decreased.

And let me offer this most important clarification, finding yourself doesn't mean you have to sever *all* ties with everyone else but rather and reassuringly so, it is about discovering who you are so that you can build and strengthen ties with those around and afar (i.e. the miner can help the blacksmith and the blacksmith can assist the swordsmen with their creations).

And so, the more we are aware of our falsehoods, the more we will be able to peel them off our beings, the more our authentic selves will come to reveal its glory in all splendid and miraculous wonder, and the more that we are able to help not only ourselves but also those around us. This is the first part of the journey to be. This is where we build the courage to be; this is where we find the place to be. Like seeds adrift on the wind, like pollen on a bee flown to the next flower, many times the seed must travel before it can appropriately take root. As to be is to be of position.

So, are we ready to further our journeys to be? Well, of course we are. In fact, true to just being, we've already made some of the most important initial steps.

CHAPTER 2
The Journey to Being

"When you have a vision of authenticity, the journey to your truest self is more easily sought out and better experienced."

THE 3 FUNDAMENTAL QUESTIONS OF BEING

The path to consistently getting to a place of being can be tricky. But there are 3 fundamental questions that help move us onward on our journeys to that of our greatest selves.

1. **Who do I not want to be?** For most, this will be the easiest out of the three questions. And while it may not put us directly on our paths to being, it allows us to be closer to it. Using the process of elimination, by knowing who we are not, we can be steered and guided into knowing who we are, which leads us to the next question.

ON THE JOURNEY OF JUST BEING

2. **Who am I Being?** No, not your name, not your title at work, not the accomplishments you have gained over the years. These are things other people have imposed on you. The question again is who am I being? Not what others have allowed or convinced you to become.

    So, what is the very definition of your essence? Who are you when no one is around? And when people are around, are you essentially the same person? Of course, you'll probably have to think about this question a little more than the previous one, as it is often more complex. For to think about who we are involves us tapping into ourselves, and it provides to us a great and conscious starting point to our wondrous present and coming journeys.

3. **Lastly, who do I want to be?** All of us growing up were used to being asked: *"what do you want to be when you grow up?"* And while there is absolutely nothing wrong with that question, it would do us all better if we get into the habit of also asking and being asked *"who do we want to be when we grow up?"*, even if we are already grown. For example, do you want to be more knowledgeable, better engaged, more punctual… truer?

The Journey to Being

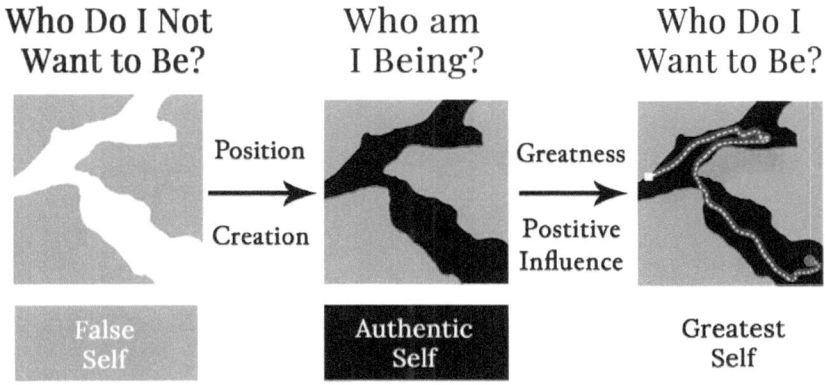

It is important to ask these questions because when you have a vision of authenticity, the journey to your truest self is more easily sought out and better experienced. When you see who you want to be or signs of it, you won't have to wonder so much if something is right or wrong for you. And at least for a period, an end goal is established, acting as a great continuous point of reference to readjust and reanalyze your next moves in life as you see them most fit.

Starting today, I encourage you to (1) answer these questions as best as you can, and (2) set a reoccurring time frame (i.e. every 3 months, every 6 months) for when you should check back and go over these questions. Don't be discouraged if you don't know all that you think you should know about your being. The journey is here for a reason and much of that reason is for us to become more knowledgeable about our beings and how they interact in the world we live in.

ON THE JOURNEY OF JUST BEING

So now that we have a better picture of our internal beings, let us learn how we can use this being to navigate our outside environments and better maintain this most powerful sense of personal fulfillment.

THE 3 EXTERNAL NAVIGATIONAL CUES

There are three essential environmental cues that help navigate us into our destinies. They are: (1) sight, (2) awareness, and (3) instinct. And as we journey through life, we are to use the three cues in conjunction with each other as much and as best as we possibly can. This way, we can be more properly guided to that of our authentic and greater selves. This way, we may be encompassed rightfully by all our internal compasses.

- **Sight** is the visuals of the world around us. It is what we can see within the limits of our perception. For example, one may see a river or a mountain in any given direction.

- **Awareness/education** acts as the body of our compass, labeling all the many directions we can travel with great accuracy. It is the set of tools we can use to better navigate our surroundings, to better measure the depth of the river or estimate the height of the mountain that we must either overcome or go around.

- And then there is **Instinct**. It is the action or inaction of the needle within our compass. It is the gravitational pull that aides us into and through our walks. Instinct gives us the

The Journey to Being

courage and decisiveness to determine if the river should be crossed or if the mountain needs to be climbed.

Keep in mind that when our visuals are faulty, and we can't judge from our vantage point just what is on the other side of the mountain or just how deep the river we are about to cross is, we must rely heavily more on our education and instinct. When our education isn't where it needs to be, and the points on the compass seem inaccurate, we are then forced to use more of our visuals and/or our instincts until our awareness is strengthened from sought knowledge.

With that said, many times we journey to unnecessary places and end up wasting a multitude of valuable time and energy because the visuals were all great but the compass as a whole was neglected. We didn't trust our instincts and the knowledge needed to read and comprehend them. And instead of following our true paths, we go in all wrong and opposite directions. But when we have all three—our visuals, our awareness and the ability to bring meaning to it, and the insightful needle of instinct, we are then allowed and encouraged to co-create our most powerful and fulfilling embodiment of being.

And while we can learn a great deal from our environment and other people, we will never get the fullest picture of our lives until we take the journey for ourselves. Again, let us not forget that to be is to be in and of position in both time and space. For if we are not consistently in the right position, in the internal state of being, our journeys in life will assist in giving us a repetition of poor results.

ON THE JOURNEY OF JUST BEING

THE REPETITION OF POOR RESULTS

When we aren't properly coursing through the path of just being, life tends to expose to us the repetition of poor results. For if we don't have a map, or don't know exactly how to read one, it is common for us to end up going in circles, touching unnecessarily the same points over and over, getting the same result and leaving little or no room for sustainable growth.

Whatever *"it"* may be, life will repeat the lesson until you decide to become a better you. Many people are ignorant of this fact, and for this reason, some attempt to be more stubborn than life can be. Such people think that they can beat life at its own benefiting game, not even taking the time to realize that it is life that holds us and allows us to be.

There is a price to pay to live, a price to pay to be. This means that all of us have some work to do. The thing is, many people are paying to be moved in the wrong directions. Then, of course, the further you are off route, the more time and energy it will take for you to get back to a sense of truth and the harder it will be for you to rediscover your authentic self, as your brain tries its best to distinguish the more familiar false self from the real you.

One must know that there are no shortcuts in life and the only cheat sheets allowed are found in the generous whispers of instinct and in the thoughtful odes of repetitious outcomes. With that said, keep in mind that the repetition of poor results is not necessarily a terrible thing. You see, such repetition occurs not as punishment but rather as a light to

The Journey to Being

show us what we, otherwise, might and do still often miss.

When we come to know the benefits of the repetition of poor results, we then have the potential to see the trials in our lives as just that, as trials, *"as tests used to evaluate and enhance one's aptness or performance in any given circumstance or lesson."*

You see, we all have been gifted with seeds; seeds that will only grow fruitful in the right conditions when we are in the right position, the right space of mind, time, and spirit to just be.

If you plant a palm tree on the side of a frigid mountain, chances are that it won't grow no matter how many times you plant it. At best, the seed just sits there waiting, dormant, as if something will happen and be long-lasting. It is nothing but a trial. But if the conditions stay unfavorable to growth, the outcome will remain the same and the repetition of poor results will ensue.

Now take that same seed and plant it in a tropical climate where all it has to do is just be. Yes, it may take some work getting there and some time will have to pass, but eventually, that seed will grow strong enough to stand the likes of hurricanes. Place a pine where it belongs, and it will eventually be able to face blizzards just as well as a cactus in a desert faces the blistering sun.

> **You see, we THRIVE when we are where and who we should be.**

You see, we thrive when we are where and who we should be, even in the midst

ON THE JOURNEY OF JUST BEING

of troubles, even surrounded by disturbances and indescribable circumstances. However, if you find yourself just sitting there, not even having found enough growth to see the totality of your being, chances are you have planted yourself and your spirit in a place not very conducive to growth.

We are a body of seeds, and we plant them in our acts, thoughts, behaviors, discoveries, and enlightenments. When we are in the right space, despite the surrounding circumstances, we grow; and if we aren't, we don't.

But once you've found an acceptable grounding…once you've found yourself, all you have to do is just be. The soil will be just right, the range in temperatures will be befitting, and the weather most often will bring to you the amount of sunshine, rain, and nutrients needed to elevate you up and into your destiny. It will be as if the world, the universe, has orchestrated itself to be a willing and serving participant in your life.

Keep in mind, too, that sometimes the repetition of poor results comes from our beings wanting to be other beings, from seeds wanting to be other seeds. Instead of enduring the intermittent frustrations of getting to the place to be, we hope that we can just bypass all aspects of growth and being and plant ourselves anywhere we see fit. Many of us visualize our seeds growing in unconducive places because, quite frankly, it is sometimes easier to imagine ourselves as other seeds than to accept and cultivate the fertile seeds we carry within.

But this type of thinking is useless. A cactus in a desert may wish

The Journey to Being

to find the moisture like the kelp in the sea, but will quickly find the swaying waves nauseatingly brutal. And the kelp may wish to find the stability of land, envious of the cactus that's been afforded the privilege of protection from hungry critters. But in the desert sun, it would wither away before its roots could even pierce the soft sand. Not to mention that no matter how hard one wishes to be another, it does not, cannot, and will not happen. If you really want to be someone else or live someone else's life, then you are missing it. You have not found the true gift of being, that your being for you is God's greatest feat.

Once you come to this realization, the world around you will sync to your motions, you will be able to sing to life and have the cheerful opportunity to listen while life echoes it back.

And to be honest, everyone will repeat mistakes at some point. Sometimes we just don't know the solutions (not to be confused with we just aren't looking for them). Sometimes, we are not even aware that a trial is among us. But the point is that we do not revel in our patterned mistakes, but become more conscious of the trials we encounter so that we can learn what is needed to move on. Just because we are seemingly positioned poorly at this moment doesn't mean we can't be positioned more properly in the next.

You see, seeds are sturdy little packets of life. They can sense their surroundings and appropriately determine what will bring their roots hardships and what will give pleasure to the form they will soon become.

ON THE JOURNEY OF JUST BEING

Therefore, seeds have become masters at conceptualizing the hardship or pleasure of perception, for they have learned to grow in their appropriate environments even if such environments aren't perfect or optimal.

THE HARDSHIP OR PLEASURE OF PERCEPTION

The journey will not always be easy, but it will not always be hard. In fact, most of the time, it remains somewhere in the middle, and it will be up to you to decide and define your own life's experience.

Let's try something. Is your life right now of hardship or pleasure? If you say it is of hardship, are there any positive aspects involved (i.e. growth, family, friends, faith, etc.)? Are there any constructive or hidden benefits? I'll go ahead and assume that there are, as it can't be *all* bad, right?

Conversely, if you say your experience is pleasurable, I'm sure there are or will be some factors involved that you'd change if you could. You see, most of the time, life and our experiences within it are what we make them.

Two people can be on the same path. For one person, this path can seem extremely daunting, but for the other, it can be extremely rewarding. For those who know that their journeys, their trials were made to benefit them, they seamlessly choose the latter. And obviously so, they are more likely to master more quickly the art of being.

But wherever your position is in life, here are nine things (in a general order of relevance) we all can do to get to and better tread the

The Journey to Being

journey of just being.

MASTERING THE JOURNEY OF BEING

1. **Pave Your Road with Courage.** There is no doubt that it takes courage to be. It will take courage to be completely honest with yourself; it will take courage to be who you are when circumstances or people wish and hope for you to needlessly change.

   Without courage, the journey will either be (1) agonizing or (2) impossible, either of which we don't want. Often, when we think of a long project or a big insurmountable journey, we try to muster up all the courage we need to complete the whole challenge as if we are to conquer it in a moment's time. But all we really need to do is consistently gather enough courage to get to and get through the next steps.

   If you feel you lack courage, here are a couple of simple ways to build it:

   - *Keep Your Goals and Checkpoints in Mind.* Once you know where you think you want to be, somehow getting there seems a little more worth it. Many times, you will need this extra push, the smile it puts on your face, and the firm ambition it sets in your mind.

   - *Dream Big.* Big dreams require courage. And once

ON THE JOURNEY OF JUST BEING

something is required, chances are people will go out, find, and obtain what is necessary to acquire it. Sometimes, when our dreams aren't big enough, excuses are more easily built, and we are less likely to take the time or energy needed to muster the courage required.

2. **Know That the Journey Will Take Time and Energy.** You are a body of seeds and sowing and harvest will often require at least a season in between.

    Do not be discouraged, time is needed for you to learn what you need to grow, and energy will be consumed so that you learn to use it wisely. You must be okay with this and know that the time and energy displaced in the work to build a better you are only expended to suit your favor. Embracing our journey allows us to acknowledge that we play a vital role in fostering such a spectacular life. It allows us to see how tough we can be while creating greater parts of our being.

3. **Know Where Your Strength Lies.** This is critical! When times get tough (and they will get tough), you will want and need to know what it is that motivates you so that you can get to and through the next stages of your life. This motivation can be your children or your spouse. This may be God and/ or your goals, or a lot of times the alternative of you not just being.

The Journey to Being

By knowing where your strength lies you can use them when you need to, as it will give you the much-needed courage when you're feeling overwhelmed or when you must deal with the oppression caused by your own debilitating fears.

4. **Declutter Your Pack Full of Fears.** It is only natural to assume that if you are on the journey to your true self, your pack may be filled with the weight of your fears. If so, it's time to unpack. It's time to get rid of those useless fears to make room to carry all the things in your life that really matter; the things that you will really need on this journey of and to self-discovery.

   As everyone knows, fear is one of the most enduring hindrances to getting to any place of success, and in the same respect, it is also a formidable opponent to being. To overcome fear, one must find the courage and strength previously discussed, but too, they must be able to distinguish and be aware of the kind of fears that they may be possibly experiencing.

   There are two types of fears: (1) Plausible or legitimate fear - the fear that may result in lethal, unethical, unlawful, and truly devastating conclusions if one acts within the confines of them, and (2) irrational fears - fears that don't rightfully have a place in one's psyche.

ON THE JOURNEY OF JUST BEING

It is bewildering, but not exactly surprising, to think that the number of irrational fears present in our lives and within our beings is comparable to the plausible fears we face. With that said, here are some of the most common irrational fears of being and what one needs to know to acknowledge their presence and successfully work through them.

- **The Fear of Failure.** Perhaps, the greatest apprehension and most frequent fear we all face in terms of being is the fear of failure. This fear, to most, is undoubtedly real and can sometimes be, without question, terrifying. But still, too many fear failures for no reason at all. And in fact, because of this, many people are already failing, ironically, solely because they fear it.

  You see, here's the thing about failure: if you fear it and decide not to act, then it, failure, is going to automatically occur because you have *failed* to try or *failed* to keep going when a fantastic opportunity has presented itself. As a result, we condemn ourselves to the very same outcome we have attempted so despairingly to avoid, and we do it without any gained growth.

  So why should we fear failure if our inaction automatically results in us failing? Such would be like saying I don't want to get my feet wet and then motion yourself into a

The Journey to Being

cannonball. Therefore, in many situations we might as well try, at least we can then take something away from the experience.

With that said, sometimes, we are able to further assess that there are only two ways to properly prevent or overcome failure: (1) be perfect (good luck with that), and (2) find the reasons why the *"error"* or *"mistake"* occurred. If we can do this, then we have done ourselves a great favor making what seemed to be a massive failure into a grand success. So many people fear failure simply because deep down inside they fear success or, worse, they fear success because their definition of it is skewed.

There is a common misconception that success only comes in the form of joy, wealth, or immense triumph, but sometimes major successes can be found amid

> There is a common misconception that success only comes in the form of joy, wealth, or immense **TRIUMPH**.

understanding and advancing through heartache, pain, and struggle. We just have to learn to tune ourselves to success' sometimes strange frequencies. We must begin to recognize this unfamiliar success if an experience wasn't exactly how we thought it would be, and we must not obtain failure solely because we chose not to find the success that often transpires from it. This would be like getting an expensive package and not taking the time to open and properly receive its value.

- *The Fear of the Unknown*. Many people will also fail to open the hypothetical package mentioned above when it comes to, perhaps, the next most prominent irrational fear, the fear of the unknown. When it comes to life and being yourself, this should not trouble you much. Who you will or might become should be in mind, but it should not worry you much because at any given point you are the only one who defines your being, no matter what circumstance it finds itself in.

If you are completely lost, then still do not be dismayed, do not agonize in any way if your most complete being doesn't come to you overnight—because it probably won't. Again, it is okay to become a better and more authentic you day by day and moment by moment, just as we seamlessly do with other, more routine activities. We won't neglect today's dinner because we don't know what we will be eating two weeks from now. Similarly, we won't stop at a green light

The Journey to Being

because we don't know if the next traffic light will be red.

The unknown should not be feared. Instead, embrace it and let the discovery, whenever and wherever appropriate, excite you. When you encounter darkness, be the light that you need to face and erase it. This is how we learn to acknowledge and enjoy the new and positive aspects of our becoming.

> The unknown should not be feared. Instead, **EMBRACE** it and let the **DISCOVERY**, whenever and wherever appropriate, excite you.

- *The Fear of Criticism*. People are going to talk about you whether you are doing something seemingly worthwhile or not, so you might as well be doing something good. Know that as you embark on your journey of being, criticism will come from many angles and varied distances. The good thing about just being is that you know or will soon come to know a lot more about who you are. And the more we know about ourselves, the less unconstructive criticisms can and will hurt us. The more we can be, the more we are able to accurately define our true selves within the guidelines of our journey's purpose and our purpose's journey, as sometimes paths in our lives are not really directed toward us.

ON THE JOURNEY OF JUST BEING

The more we know ourselves, the greater the likelihood we will want to better ourselves, and the better we become at filtering, at deciding what will help us along the way and what will not.

In saying that, it is wise to know what true constructive criticism is and what it is not. Constructive criticism comes from a place of positivity and purpose. It judges actions but not so much the person who made them, and it gives the receiver space to find their own way in their own time. With that said, your actions are ultimately your choice. If you choose not to listen, then that is your decision, and that is okay. But too, think about and be willing and ready to face the consequences of your choices whether they are what you expect or something worse or better.

Unconstructive criticism, or *"hating"* as the word embodies, often comes from a place of hate, jealousy, ignorance, or ridicule. It often judges the person more than their actions and more often than not, it is worded in a way that does not convey growth or prosperity to its receiver. Unconstructive criticism hates; it attempts to tear us apart. Constructive criticism builds; it attempts to make us stronger.

- **The Fear of Non-acceptance and Disappointing Others.** We must accept that everyone we love and come to know will

The Journey to Being

not understand what is best for us and/or why we do things a certain way.

Naturally, after disagreeing to change ourselves, our first instincts are to try to change the minds of those close to us. If you are persuasive or supported enough, you may succeed. But if you are not, then they will end up trying to change your mind while you try to change theirs, and both parties may not achieve much. This, undoubtedly, will have led to frustrations and many times that person or persons disappointed in you will equate your frustrations to your decision to be, and not more appropriately so to their misunderstandings of your being, or the journey of it.

If they don't choose to at least try to understand, then that is their choice. If you have not harmed them purposely and without apologies, if necessary, then there is only one thing you can do: Just be. Be happy for you and the being on its path. It is easy for us to say that *"this"* is a good decision but go and show them why *"it"* is, if it is, in fact, authentic. Go the extra mile and show others why being of love, truth, and forgiveness is what's essentially best for you and everyone you encounter.

- ***Lastly, is The Fear of Commitment***. Commitment, I believe, is quite natural to us. Such is evident from our stubborn routines, which wouldn't exist nearly as much without it. Just think about it, we all have habits (both good and bad). And what would a habit, instinctual or learned, be without some large level of commitment? On the other hand, I'm also certain that all of us are committed in some fashion or another not to engage in certain actions or behaviors. So why is it that many of us are still, on some level or another, afraid of commitment?

Well, the fear of committing is just an indication or compilation of the other fears. If you have the fear of commitment, chances are you have another fear, most likely one or more of the fears mentioned previously. For instance, the fear of the unknown and a fear of failure may give rise to a fear to commit to a relationship. As a result, instead of realizing the associated fears, we often trick ourselves into thinking that commitment is the real issue.

It is also good to note that there is indeed a difference between fearing commitment and not being or feeling able to commit. Although this book will not cover the latter in much detail, I can tell you this. Practice being committed to yourself. Do things that are healthy, that promote a future of happiness and bring joy to you without harming others.

When we are authentically committed to ourselves, we are

The Journey to Being

actively participating in being, and in addition, we can be more apt and more appropriately committed to others. We have to find this commitment in ourselves first, recognize it, practice it, and then allow ourselves to be it until the fear of commitment turns into a nothingness, until the fog removes itself to make way for the clarity of one's grand being, as then are we able to more greatly keep our visions in sight.

5. ***Keep Your Vision in Sight.*** If you want to get to where you're going, keep your focus by always holding your visions close to you, even when they indeed feel far away. There are a lot of distractions in life, and on your journey, you may come into circumstances where you may not understand what is going on or why it involves you. Keep your pace steady and your eyes on the progression of your growth.

    We often focus so much on the bad things that we miss a lot of opportunities to focus on and have joy in the good things, even if they had not yet come to pass. Know that your dreams are always in reach, not that they have been or will be fully realized, but because at any moment you can at least partially be of them. Feel them, really feel them building up inside of you. Feel them in your heartbeat, touch them as if they are your skin, immerse yourself in them and eventually some, all, and many times more portions than you could ever imagine will come to pass.

Also, realize your small successes. Begin to recollect all the things you can do when and if you just put your mind to it. Remind yourself daily of all your successes, and you, too, will more easily find the drive to keep going.

6. **Keep Your Brain Conscious and Your Eyes Open.** Getting to and growing yourself on your journey, of course, can and will be challenging, but there is so much more to gain from life when we can first acknowledge and mentally get past our obstacles.

   You see, keeping your brain conscious and your eyes open has many purposes. Aside from steering us clear from danger, conscious living can reveal to us (1) the multitude of ways we can enjoy our journeys and (2) explain purposely just what our journeys are all about. Consciousness is where knowledge is gathered and where instincts are honed. It is such mindful intake that allows our beings to not only face our situations, but in addition, show us that the essences of our beings are not constructed with the bricks and mortar of our problems.

   In contrast, it is often consciousness that allows us to break from our issues by letting us know that we are not of them.

7. **Know That You Are Not Your Environment.** When walking on the path to a greater self, one of the most important things to realize is that you are not your struggles. You are not the

The Journey to Being

contours of your journey. Instead, you are most often merely passing through them. Many times, instead of just being and getting through our

> **❝**
> We let our trails **BE**come our trials instead of turning our trials into trails.

journeys, we instead opt to embody them. We let our trails become our trials instead of turning our trials into trails. Many times, instead of moving past our problems, we blindly and more readily take them up.

For we tread and we trek, but the paths we may never physically become, for only in our thoughts can we imagine embodying them, and only in our thoughts can we truly manifest our path's tremendous weight, turning them, as we sometimes do, into a host of overwhelming feelings. We may seem one with our paths, but it is our beings that know, crave, and excel at being greater than one often realizes they are. It is our beings that know, without a doubt,

> **❝**
> It is our **BE**ings that know, without a doubt, that we are meant to move and be **MOVED**.

that we are meant to move and be moved, and not to be moved on and stepped over as, of course, we often allow ourselves to be.

49

ON THE JOURNEY OF JUST BEING

So many times on our paths, we run into deep trenches of emotions, mountainous situations, and unexpected detours, and instead of being and allowing ourselves to pour out and expand to overcome and move past our troubles, we, instead, begin to pull ourselves down to collect the very same environment we so eagerly wish to leave. For here is what we do.

We travel on our paths and occasionally, as people do, we trip. And then we say, well, if I pick up this rock (or whatever it is that brings us down), then I won't ever have to trip over this particular item again. We say, let me keep this shame and this guilt so that I will never make this mistake again. And as we trip again and again, as imperfect humans do, we gather and we gather and we gather.

And instead of just being and floating above our downers, we drown ourselves in pools of our own self-cultivating emotions. Instead of just being and climbing over and around our mountains, we drag boulders of doubt, complaints, excuses, and self-pity. And instead of just being and using the best of the paths life has given us, we try instead to hack and weed through our own original and stubbornly-solidified plans.

We must understand and acknowledge that we choose to mentally carry hatred, shame, pity, guilt, an unhealthy self-

The Journey to Being

consciousness, illnesses, and issues. This is because when we have the profound and powerful insight to know that we do hold our spiritual weight, we then more greatly gain the ability to let such harmful inessentials go.

This doesn't mean we won't ever feel or face life's sorrows as they are also a part of our journeys. It means we can let them stay on the journey where they belong and not invite them within the confines of our own moving and esteemed selves.

When we are just being, we can appropriately disassociate ourselves mentally, physically, and spiritually from our journey's struggles, and even in the midst of hardship, we can keep the souls of our beings light.

8. **Know that it is Okay and Sometimes Appropriate to Change Courses.** Knowing that it is okay to change paths when it favors our journey of just being is key when traveling en route to our true and greater selves. We must remember that our beings are what move us. And to keep our sense of being, we must move with it. We must align and center ourselves with it, for that is where we will find our balance again, that is where we will find once more a more apparent version of our authentic selves.

But to access the truer self, we must first peel our layers of falseness.

ON THE JOURNEY OF JUST BEING

9. **Peeling Away the False Layers of Self.** The false layers of the self are like unnecessary layers of clothes. And when people have so many on, not only do they find it hard to move, but they can hardly be moved. They are so rigid with their ways of life. And while they may show that they have access to luxuries, it doesn't help them, as one becomes less and less familiar with the touch of their own natural skin.

   The heaviest and most outer layer of unnecessary clothing is the ego. If the ego isn't ended, then the mind won't often properly process what exactly you need to fix or get rid of, and how then can you go about taking on the feats of not being?

   We can think of the ego as a coat. Yes, it may temporarily keep us from feeling cold as it hides all the other layers of falsehood underneath. And yes, it may feel nice and comfy to wear, but all too often it also keeps us from acknowledging and confidently creating our own inner warmth.

Once the ego is gone, we are more apt and able to take off all the other layers of falsehood, all of such that keeps us from the touch of ourselves, all of such that keeps us from being. The next chapter shows us just how we can begin to erode and erase our egos, one of the most important steps as we continue our journeys of just being.

CHAPTER 3
Erasing the Ego

> *"One must be aware that our ego's version of confidence can only imitate; it is only a mirror, a reflection. It is a mockery of confidence because real confidence takes work, it just doesn't show up."*

THE THREE MAJOR LIES OF THE EGO

The reason ego is noted first is because it encourages us to block our authentic selves by covering up all the other more minor layers of falsehood. It tells us that we are perfect and that our beings need little to no growth at all. As a result of our ego's veil, we often fail to see the issues of our beings by pretending that they are not there, even when we know for certain that they are.

Often, we think that if we possess an ego, which acts, of course, to better our moods and fill the voids of our lost confidence, then others will see us in the same glorious manner we see ourselves in. And sometimes, for particular audiences, it works for at least the moment. But

ON THE JOURNEY OF JUST BEING

what makes being egotistic stand out among the other mechanisms of falsehood is that it has the ability to not only distort your current self but eventually make you feel as if such distortion is of reality. You see, when we wear egotism, we wear masks that are adorned. And while many times they are captivating to witness and take in, they are not nearly as majestic and genuine as our own appealing embodiment.

It is the ego that moves us quickly out of our authentic selves and into a wave of false perception, and it does so with three self-telling lies.

1. The first lie it tells the individual is: *"I have a bountiful amount of confidence."* It makes a person feel empowered, but fills them up with air instead of substance, and places them on unsteady pedestals where they are often not prepared or knowledgeable enough to balance their misappropriated placement.

2. The second lie it tells the individual is: *"I am better than others."* It does this in several ways, but mostly so when money, attention, power, status, and *"stuff"* comes into play. It tells the individual that because they possess such items, characteristics, or demeanors, they are worthier than another. Of course, as all lies are defined, this just isn't true. True worth does not come from attention or *"stuff,"* as it is not so much about adding objects on but rather bringing and spreading out our true essence. It's about being of worth instead of just trying to portray it.

3. The third self-destructing lie the ego tells an individual is:

Erasing the Ego

"I have already reached portions of my greatest self," when they undoubtedly know that this is not true. This is, of course, bad because if one already thinks that they have reached their greatest self and they haven't, they'll logically tend to abandon their true authentic self for a false short-lived sense of accomplishment. Their false sense of being says to them that they have done enough, that they have made it, while their authentic self would have honestly told them that they could do, could be, better. And instead of progressing, they get, at least for the moment, well, stuck.

Just think of the Greek tragedy of Narcissus from which the term narcissism or the extreme excessive love of the self originates. Narcissus was a mythological man awestruck by his own physical attributes. He was lured to the pond where he was so perplexed by his highly admirable reflection that his stare became permanent as he failed to see the reflection as nothing less than an image.

Narcissus was so into the false sense of his self that he totally forgot and ignored the state of his actual being. He died staring at his false self as so many of us do both literally and figuratively. You see, our egos can be dangerous, and they have the ability to make us do things our normal beings just wouldn't do, especially when we

> **❝** You see, you cannot authentically just **BE** when your being is not **AUTHENTIC**.

ON THE JOURNEY OF JUST BEING

have not known or haven't identified just who our natural, authentic beings are.

You see, you cannot authentically just be when your being is not authentic.

In order to better understand the dynamic trio of confidence, ego, and humility, one must grasp the concept of how they all relate. In order to create the right type of humility, get rid of the ego, and move your being into a higher power of confidence. Here is what you need to understand about the cycle the three compose.

THE CYCLE OF CONFIDENCE, EGO, AND HUMILITY

The cycle of confidence, ego, and humility is important because it shows us how each factor relates to the others in the grand scheme of our beings. Keep in mind that the direction and speed in which one may move all depend on time, experience, and, most importantly, will.

Erasing the Ego

1. **The Cycle Moves Both Ways, Except in One Area.** And that is at the very top position between that of your highest state of being and your ego.

    Yes, it is fairly easy to fall from a high place of confidence to that of an ego, but it is impossible for one to go directly from that of ego to a high self-assured being. This gap is just too distant. In these instances, to get back to a place of confidence, however timely, one must go through (at varied speeds) both types of humility.

    Ego ↔ Shameful Humility ↔ Gracious Humility ↔ Confidence → Ego

2. **In Between Ego and Confidence Lives Humility, and It Comes in Two Different Forms.** Shameful humility, which resides closer to ego, is often exploited by our egos to bring our beings back to it. No one enjoys humiliation, and sometimes a quick *"fix"* of pride may seem like what our uncomfortable beings need to be consoled back into a selfish egotism.

    But there is another way, and that is to stop being shameful and to start being grateful. Gracious humility brings life to our beings, while shameful humility, at the very best, adds nothing. While shameful humility acknowledges the disconnect from self, it is gracious humility that acknowledges our vision and allows us to see all that we truly embody. Gracious humility moves opposite from its counterpart. It wants us to do and be better, and for that reason, it often succeeds in helping us reach our authentic selves and also our highest places of confidence.

3. **The truth is, Our Egos Make Us Less Bold Than What We Often Perceive.** By pretending to foster the confidence our beings crave, the ego gives us so much false confidence. It convinces our being that it is worthy of being taken up. But one must be aware that our ego's version of confidence can only imitate; it is only a mirror, a reflection. It is a mockery of confidence because real confidence takes work, it just doesn't show up.

4. **The Falls Will Differ.** Because we are humans, we will fall on both sides of the cycle, while strengthened in confidence and/or immersed in ego. Fortunately, on the confidence side, we don't fall nearly as far. Yes, it may still hurt, and we may still be disappointed, but it's nothing compared to that of our egos' crashing.

When our egos go down, it often shatters what we thought of as our true being. Because of such shock, many of us in these moments feel betrayed by ourselves. But often, it is in these moments that ourselves offer to us a gift. Such a fall is breaking away layers of falseness to expose the real you. It offers us the opportunity to build ourselves in the fortifying ways of confidence, and away from the true frailty of our egos, strengthening us so that we do not break so harshly in our

Erasing the Ego

future falls in life.

5. Lastly, **The Ego is Not Needed.** Perhaps, the most surprising thing to know is that when one reaches an aspect of their greatest selves they will realize that the ego is not even remotely necessary to feel alive and to be fulfilled, that the highest state of being doesn't even fall within the realm of the ego but within the sound, beautiful explosion of love and purpose that is the self in its truest form of confidence.

As you can see from the diagram, and I'm sure you have witnessed from firsthand experiences, sometimes, it is easy to think that we are displaying confidence when, in fact, we have fallen for the devious coaxing of our egos. For those who aren't well aware of the differences between their assured authentic self and their ego, the next section highlights the sometimes-blurred line between them.

THE DIFFERENCES BETWEEN EGO AND ESTEEM

There is often a thin line between confidence and its sometimes-imitating emotion, ego. But with three simple questions, one can honestly assess if they are truly authentic or more so arrogant. So, ask yourself:

1. **Who Am I Ultimately Serving?** This, perhaps, is the most telling question. In other words, what are you using your energy for? Is it solely

or mostly for yourself, or is it also being used to bring out the greatness in others?

Keep in mind, the question is who are you ultimately serving? You see, a lot of times and accurately so, we must make ourselves feel good before extending such positive energy onto others. This is usually done with confidence. However, when ego is involved, this great feeling normally stops with the self, the self who just wants to be seen, acknowledged, and revered by all others.

2. **Am I Putting Stuff Over Self?** The ego loves the portrayal of the false self, and it often uses stuff as well as attention to express this adoration. The ego likes stuff because it (1) helps to conceal the authentic self and (2) offers a distraction while it builds a gradual sense of falseness, both to the individual who holds the ego and also to the individuals that surround them.

And let's be honest, *"stuff"* in many ways is a part and will forever be a part of our lives. And, of course, there is no disgrace in that. The dishonoring of the authentic self comes when people start to forget about the self to grasp, idolize, and uphold above all other stuff. That is when we begin to forget our true and becoming selves.

3. **Lastly, ask yourself, What Is It That I Am Seeking?** What is it you wish to gain after such a powerful and magnificent

Erasing the Ego

feeling enters you? And what do you wish to gain after that feeling has dissipated from you?

Many times, the ego will only wish to seek attention for itself. It will seek for those to be jealous or envious of us, and it will seek a bounteous amount of self-worth, while, oddly enough, demanding little to nothing from ourselves in return. Ironically, it is the ego that subconsciously seeks a level of confidence. It seeks purpose in one's self. Because of this, those that harbor an ego tend to feel as if they can never have enough of it. And often, instead of seeking true confidence, they attempt and often obtain more ego, thus filling the void of their lack of confidence with purposeless space.

With that said, if you are seeking growth, integrity, will, inspiration, or any other virtuous characteristic you too are seeking (more) confidence. And the truer the confidence you have, the less ego you will feel you need and the more you will know that you have what it takes to boldly just be on such paths.

One of the hardest actions for those who are used to carrying an ego is to carry the thoughts of having to leave this glorious perception of themselves behind. Coated in their false sense of security, many egotistic people actually lack confidence—the strength it takes to be vulnerable enough to face their real self. And unfortunately, or fortunately so

ON THE JOURNEY OF JUST BEING

depending on the situation, many people do not wish to do this, or don't think that they can handle their authentic selves until an eye-opening life event forces them to do so.

For those that are attached to their ego, there will be times when the pond you stare so deeply into becomes rippled. It will then show you the self that you have or will become if you do not let go of such a fraudulent persona.

You either leave the ego or waste your time waiting for the day the walls of such falseness come down…because eventually, they will come down.

But the remarkable thing is, once you let the ego go (and notice I didn't say once the ego lets you go), you'll give yourself the grand reality of not just where you are on your journey of just being but where you soon could be and who you could soon become. Here is how you build a true and strengthening confidence without having to embody the false almighty ego.

BUILDING CONFIDENCE APART FROM EGO

Because our truths are bound to light, your ego, as long as you sustain it, will eventually and continually be an ever-coming disappointment. You will never be able to live up to its grandness. And because it requires so much to maintain an overstated self, sooner or later the well will run dry, and the reflection will evaporate, leaving you with, well, you.

Erasing the Ego

You see, your authentic self can be ignored, but it can never be completely buried or washed away. The longer we wear our masks, the more uncomfortable they become, and the more they will itch for us to take them off.

> ❝ The longer we wear our masks, the more uncomfortable they **BECOME**, and the more they will itch for us to take them off.

So, if you want to build up your confidence apart from gathering ego, here is what you can do in 3 steps.

1. **Acknowledge and Dispose of Your Ego.** Confidence cannot be found in the ego any more than darkness can be found in light. You see, confidence is created upon the precipice of vulnerability, and accurately so, not much vulnerability can be found in anyone's ego.

    And when we think of vulnerability, we should not think of it as a weakness. We must think of it as a stepping stone to our greater selves. You see, in the same way one cannot be fearless without fear and one cannot be courageous without a challenge, one cannot build up confidence without the sheer bravery found in one's vulnerability.

2. **Just Be…Over and Over Again.** The more we learn to just be on our journeys, the more confident we tend to grow. The more we see that we are indeed able to do what our hearts

ON THE JOURNEY OF JUST BEING

desire, the more such actions will come to pass, each turn yielding more and more confidence. The same confidence that can and will be used to further our beings into their destiny.

> **You can never really LIVE up to YOUR ego's perception of YOU.**

In contrast, you can never really live up to your ego's perception of you, as such is equivalent to trying to consistently make a lie the truth. With a grandiose ego, you will always feel on top but will always have only one direction to go…and that is down. Thus, such falsehood is counter-intuitive and unrealistic to the development of one's confidence, for how can you be encouraged to progress when the only direction you could ever really go in this state of mind is below you?

Confidence, unlike ego, does not come from pretending that our challenges aren't there. Confidence comes from realizing our being's challenges and dealing with and triumphing over them with great appropriateness and strength of consciousness.

3. **Maintain and Prolong Your Sense of Being by Doing the Work to Be.** To just be is great. But like all things that are worthwhile, we do require work. No child is born without gestation. Few purposes have a successful implementation without plans, and no skill is properly crafted without training

Erasing the Ego

and the willed diligence to triumph over moments of defeat. It is this very pattern of growth that allows us to understand why and how our beings excel. We most often subconsciously work to breathe, we learn to work deeply for love and our relationships, and just as such, we must work in and within truth to just be, for work is an underlying premise of life. But so in return, when done properly, it allows us to live and it encourages us to thrive beyond our current steps.

The more work we do, the more we move to our centers, and the more we can identify and properly be within the notions of our true selves. This work is not designed to hinder us but rather it does quite the opposite. And the more work that we do to better ourselves, the more the work starts to feel less like actual work and more like the massive fulfillment of just being. Furthermore, many times, to the likeness of our journey of just being, the *"work"* needed is simply just to be, literally, to rest and be still in the splendid awareness of our limitless magnificence.

The next chapter is all about the work we must do to find ourselves and to excavate our inner truths. Only by removing the layers of falsehood can we uncover the exuberance and balance that line and live in the core of our journey. Only when can we defy the many falsehoods of our existences can we begin to develop in the fluidity of the true and grand embodiment that is ourselves in its most genuine form.

CHAPTER 4
The Development of The True Self

> *"When you compete with yourself, you automatically better your chances at winning in life, as when you compete with yourself you are automatically destined to win."*

THE CROSSINGS OF COMPARISON

The development of the true self comes directly from the abandonment of the false self, and the abandonment of the false self comes foremost from our acknowledgment of it.

As we've seen with the ego, there are many ways one can pick up and live under false layers of self. This can be initiated or exacerbated with drama, the illusory reward of falsehood, the overpowering impersonation of our virtual selves, unhealthy escaping mechanisms, faulty competitiveness, and a strand of harsh methodologies based on comparison.

You see, for us to become more authentic, we need to understand

ON THE JOURNEY OF JUST BEING

just how we are influenced by our own thinking and that of those around us.

Broadly speaking, there are four different ways in which people are normally persuaded by themselves and others to leave their truth and enter some level of falsehood in relation to comparison. Using the diagram shown, you can cross the axes (from left to top) to determine the given circumstance.

1. **You Wanting You to Be Like Others.** This is just another fancy, more general way of saying that you don't want to be like yourself.

    "My life is so boring."

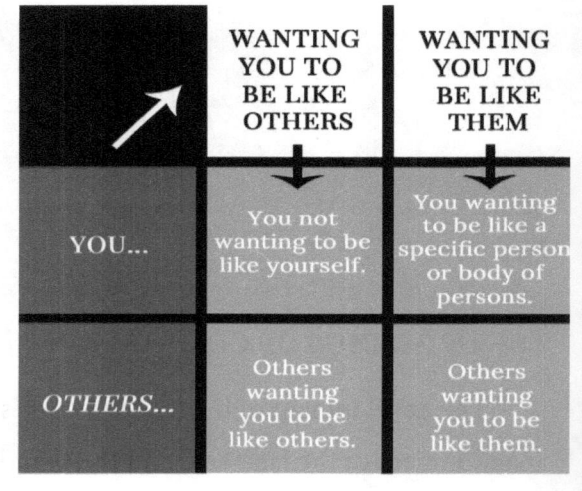

"My life isn't what it used to be."

"Oh, how I wish I was someone else."

This rhetoric is so common and repetitive that most of the time we don't even realize what it is that we are really saying. As a result, this is the subconscious message we deliver to ourselves over and over again. We encourage a false sense of

The Development of the True Self

self and don't even acknowledge that we are doing so. And so at these times, we must ask ourselves, how can we journey on our paths to just being when we want so surely in these moments to be someone else?

Solely recognizing the discomfort in your life will not make things better. Remembering being is essentially both a noun and a verb, so hoping when something can be done is a waste of time and energy. Wishing you were someone else will not make your situations, problems, or even your boredom disappear, and it most certainly will not bring you closer to a greater sense of self. You see, wishing does little when compared to the proactive commitment of just being.

2. **You Wanting You to Be Like Them.** This refers to you wanting to be like a particular person or a particular subgroup of persons.

   "Oh, if I was as skinny as her..."

   "I'd be much cooler if I was him."

   Of course, it's okay to share characteristics with others, not to mention admire and compliment. The problem occurs when we begin to neglect ourselves and our desires to find our true beings while admiring those around us, as if both can't be done simultaneously.

   We live in a society where we ritualize and revere celebrities

ON THE JOURNEY OF JUST BEING

and other prominent figures. We want to be and live like many of them so much. We scream for them, invest in their thoughts and manifestations, we change our schedules around for them, we acknowledge their work habits, and we share with them their successes. When our sports team loses, we feel their loss almost as if we played and got defeated ourselves. And when they win, we feel the rumble of their victory. It means more to us when our spirits are joined with theirs, and there is absolutely nothing wrong with that.

But we must also ask ourselves when we take account of our own lives, are we cheering (at least on the inside) as if we are one of our own favorite people? Are we investing time and money in ourselves and in what we need to grow? Are we appreciating our own work ethic and paying attention to and celebrating our own successes however small they may be? When we have lost ourselves for a moment, had a setback, or made a mistake, do we remain loyal to our sense of being as much as we stick with our favorite teams after they have just been demolished?

As we celebrate the triumphs of others, we must find our beings and hold close our greater selves so that we may reach our own goals, so that we may find ways to cultivate partnerships, so that the success in our lives and in this world doesn't seem so unequally one-sided.

The Development of the True Self

3. Then, **There Are Others Wanting You to Be Like Others.** These are the people who are consistently comparing or contrasting you to others.

   "You should be more like [name]."

   "[Name] would never do something like this."

   This often occurs because some people think that the only way to show success is through the achievements of others. And while we can learn a great deal from others, many of us are just plain ignorant of the vast treasures that lie buried within us and even more ignorant of the varied and unique ways for which these personal prizes can be excavated.

   Many mean well. But to those receiving the criticism, it can be exceptionally frustrating as a lot of times the receiver, lost in the concept of the comparison, will focus more on trying to be like the other person than trying to master their own gifted genuineness.

   Because of this, many times such vernacular harms the person they intend to help. And instead of the receiver hearing *"this is who you should be modeling (in some form or another)"*, they often falsely hear *"I am not enough"* or *"my own being is not capable."*

   Duly noted, it is important when engaging in conversations that may lead to such negative connotations that one remain conscious of what they take in and how they interpret it. It is okay to use others as a guide, but it is not okay to leave your truest being in doing so. Often, oddly enough, the things that make us different are the very same things that propel us into our own unique personal and public stardom.

4. Lastly, there will be plenty of **Others Wanting You to Be Like Them.** It is common for other people to want you to be like them. Parents, for example, are perhaps the first to throw onto their children their own achieved and unrealized activities and goals.

Similarly, some want to see if their dreams can be realized through another, which can be great if the two parties truly share an authentic dream. But, sometimes people just need validation that they did or are doing the right things the right way. And other times people just assume that if it worked so astoundingly well for them, you too would yield the same results, which, of course, is not always the case, as people and situations change parallel to time.

Whether the intent is selfish or selfless, one must find their center and make wise judgment calls based on, of course, their visuals, their instinct, and the span of their knowledge as it pertains to their beings and one's life paths and journeys.

It is easy to see how just one of these factors can throw off someone's persona, but when all four circumstances are happening at

The Development of the True Self

once, you can imagine how easy it could be for one to lose him or herself to comparison. For such comparison is just a faulty informal version of competition.

THE FAULTS OF COMPETITION

Competition is, in part, ingrained in every culture. The world's countries long to win the world cup and even distant tribes hold rituals that test the drive and will of their people.

Naturalist Charles Darwin noted that the natural world is filled with competition between the same and different types of organisms. But too, it should be noted that nature, using its awesome power to converge into something bigger, stronger, and smarter, is also a prominent beacon of cooperation. Birds flock, fish school, and the hoofed herd to serve as protection for both the individual and their community.

In contrast, the overall concept of competition is to be better than someone else at any given measure, and it does come with its benefits too when appropriately used. It pushes those past their limits and it inspires many to do better and achieve more. But competition, if one is not conscious of its pitfalls, can lead one into a whirlwind of personal dishonesty. It can act as a cause for one to lose their true self to the need to be revered by others. It can also lead one into a pool of negativity by allowing one to fall into the habit of putting others down just so they could feel (and not necessarily be) elevated.

Therefore, we must get to a point in our lives where we realize

ON THE JOURNEY OF JUST BEING

that we can be our own individual far better than we can be anyone else. When it comes to our authenticity, we have to get into a pattern of competing only with our falsehoods, challenging ourselves to become better people, better than the person not so much aside, in front of, or behind us, but better than the person we were in the days or even moments before.

Your life is not a race; it is not a competition. Your being, your dreams are yours, and no one but you can take them away. Do not be so eager to reach the heights of another, as then we often settle just because on some level we've felt we've won. Not that we've found the next step in our greater selves but because we've made it past someone else's greater sense of self as it relates to us. And while we aim so diligently to reach the heights of another's authenticity, we often settle below that of our own potential. We, in our waves of ego and the prestige of attention, begin to fail to realize that our greater self yields faulty results when it is calibrated using the means and the results of others.

Competing with your false you is the only sure way you can maximize your potential. When you are focused on self-competing, you can pay attention to what you need to accomplish, and you

> ❝
> Competing with your false you is the only sure way you can **MAZIMIZE YOUR POTENTIAL.**

The Development of the True Self

can establish goals that are customized to your own destiny. When you compete with yourself, you automatically better your chances at winning in life, as when you compete with yourself you are automatically destined to win. For there are many treasures to be found when we can literally mind and bring forth from mind our own businesses.

LITERALLY, MINDING OUR OWN BUSINESSES

Now, I know it is terribly irrational for me or any other person to completely stay out of everyone else's drama, but we should be at least conscious of what we speak about and take in, and the frequency and duration at which we are engaging outside of our own being for non-productive matters.

The age of *"reality"* television and the explosion of cyber self-made celebrity mills have many of us glued to the drama of people, many of those whom we don't even know. We are drawn to gossip and rumors, and the words of scandals coat our tongues for fewer reasons than growth. And often, as a result, we sit and watch other people live out their dreams while we struggle just to ponder the plausibility and implementation of our own.

And so, it seems that if the ego is the false character within us, then drama, as it is so popularly defined, is often the vessel, the stage, the platform where all the false characters come out to act. And let's face it, we've all and will at times play in life's shorts, plays, documentaries, and feature films, so these words are not out of judgment. Paying attention unselfishly to our needs is rather an act of awareness allowing us to see how minding our own business can help benefit our authenticity.

Why are we so personally drawn to the object of other peoples' lives in negative ways? Why can't we just mind our own business so that we can literally and consciously put to mind and motion our own business? Why so much drama?

1. The most obvious reason we engage in unnecessary drama is because **We Think It Won't, Can't, or Doesn't Affect Us.** But at some level and at some point, it will and does. And it may not necessarily harm us all the time per se, but one must also ask *"is it helping?"* Ask yourself how can you mind your own business if your mind isn't on it?

    Not to mention all the subconscious effects of persistently delving into drama's realm. Is there not a concern when our brains are linking drama with a false sense of value over and over again? Is there not a concern when we are actively and consistently viewing or speaking on someone's life without great benefit. Is there not a concern that we continually tell our brains that the exhausting drama and troubles of others are more significant than our own? How else do you think many of these *"dramatic"* people gained such an *"elevated"* level of societal success in the first place? How else do you think that many of us are still in the same stagnant spot?

2. Often, when we engage in unnecessary drama, **We Begin to**

The Development of the True Self

Believe That Drama Is Somewhat Equivalent to Personal Significance. For it is here we won't have to feel invisible. Here, someone will inevitably see us, even if it's not in the best light.

As a result, excessive drama often pushes us and others away from ourselves so that we may continually dress our false characters, so that we will have enough perceived stardom to put food on the table and feed the hunger of our egos. And we perform and perform until, like every great actor, that character eventually becomes us.

3. Because, **Drama Is What One Is Used To.** In such a case, we become yet more acceptable to be of it and it becomes a lot easier to live in.

There are those whose comfort zone is bounded by the atmosphere of drama. This is where they are strangely at ease, not exactly because such drama is fun or even entertaining but the thought of it not being around is even more frightening.

If we are consistently customizing our lives to view, construct, and invite and

> **❝**
> The more you mock the thought of someone else's pity, the easier it will be to **EMBRACE** the thought of **YOU**r own.

entertain drama, of course, it's going to come waltzing in. And then it's only a matter of time before the tumultuous amount of everyone else's *"stuff"* becomes yours.

The more you mock the thought of someone else's pity, the easier it will be to embrace the thought of your own. The more you scorn the failures of others, the less conscious and harsher you will be when disdaining your own. The more you subjectively judge others unfairly and without good reason, the more self-conscious in unhealthy ways you too will become.

There is an equal and opposite effect and the more we live in drama, the more it begins to live in us, and the more it becomes a false definition of our self and the personas used to describe it.

4. When we engage in unnecessary drama, **We Tend to Use the State of Other People's Problems to Make Our Own Lives Seem Better.**

   "Did you see what she/he did? I would never!"

The problem with always looking *"below"* to gauge the level of our beings is that there is where we often leave the bar; it is there where we often set the standard for our own beings.

If you are going to be looking down, it should be to lift someone up. If you're going to engage in someone's business, be engaged in someone's genuine business. I promise you, you

The Development of the True Self

will feel just as good, if not better, and at least you're bound to get something real and useful from the experience.

5. When we engage in unnecessary drama, **We Can Subconsciously Use Drama/Peoples' Businesses to Soothe Our Own Victimhood.** Sometimes, we use other peoples' issues to rationalize and normalize our own.

"If [name] is going through the same thing, then this must be at least somewhat normal. Then our beings, perhaps, were made to be this way."

Yes, in life our individual beings will have commonalities, but these similarities should be used as a tool for support, as a way to boost and inspire such likenesses to betterment. Instead, sometimes, we tend to use them as a crutch.

We cannot allow other peoples' business or drama to negatively affect the way we handle ours. Again, we must set our own standards and focus on our own pace in life.

If you have fallen victim to any of life's malignancies, don't let another being's will or outcome keep you at a place of victimhood. Your authentic self does not and will not reside in such a place for long. Instead, make it your business to persevere in all ways possible. Make it your business to use your or anyone else's struggles as a platform to victory…not victimhood.

ON THE JOURNEY OF JUST BEING

6. **We Frequently Engage in Drama Simply Because Other People Do.** If you constantly hang around people that gossip a lot, chances are you are probably going to want to contribute. Few people are comfortable feeling left out of what has become, it seems, a growing societal norm.

   This is one reason why it is important for us to take some time out to just be with ourselves. Don't let another person be the reason why you haven't found your authentic self. Yes, other people's lives can be entertaining, but there is nothing entertaining about not having a life of your own.

7. Lastly and overall, when we engage in unnecessary drama, **We Are Not Literally Minding Our Own Business.** Plain and simple, with really no other way to put it, when you're thriving in your being, you really don't have time to wallow around in everyone else's mess. Instead of us being weighted and overwhelmed with drama, when we are truly minding our own business, we are paving the path to our journeys of just being, we are improving our own business functions and the frame of our own networks. When we truly engage in being, we are focused

> **"**
> When we truly engage in being, we are focused on **KEEP**ing our beings consistently and sufficiently in **ORDER**.

The Development of the True Self

on keeping our beings consistently and sufficiently in order.

With that said, if you find yourself always in other people's business, it's most likely that you aren't doing enough; it is most likely that you have just too much time on your hands!

You see, it is impractical to find our authentic selves if we are always putting on a show solely in the name of drama. And it is nearly impossible to just be while always being enveloped in the chaos of everyone else.

Many times, too, we see the short-lived or illusory value in our falsehoods. And instead of perceiving them as costly, we acknowledge the perceived gratification in them, and much like with drama, we begin to characterize the totality of our falsehoods as rewarding.

THE ILLUSORY REWARD OF SELF-FALSEHOOD

Apart from drama and our egos, there are many ways in which our lives can lead us deceptively into thinking that our false selves are the most beneficial form of existence. For instance, a cheater in a competition can be easily treated like a true winner and, as a result, he or she may think that they are only deceiving their opponents and onlookers. But when they are fully conscious, they'll realize their greatest deception was their own being's betrayal, that they were most dishonest to themselves.

In such a case of personal knavery, we often, instead and more pleasingly so, focus on the rewards gathered, whether they be of pride, attention, money, or social status. And even though we may be gaining something, this doesn't necessarily mean we are profiting. We must be aware of what our behaviors and habits are actually costing or paying us. We have to make sure that we are not losing our authenticity buying overly-priced perishables.

It is worth saying that while many of the following deceptions are harmless, overall, they do paint a beautiful picture of reward that often drives us away from the ultimate glory of our truest selves. Over time, most of us have made this illusory behavior quite normal. Children begin to hide from their wrongdoings by lying almost as soon as they can form a real sentence. By the time we've grown up we have become professionals at telling a multitude of lies, including those that include the words and phrases *"I'm sorry"*, *"will do"*, *"okay"*, *"be right back"*, *"I'm almost there"*, and *"I didn't mean to"*. Sometimes, we aren't even fully conscious of what we are saying. And that could be because it works. For the vast majority of the time, our lies aren't even perceived, acknowledged, questioned, or ridiculed by their receivers.

Because of this, many *"professional"* politicians become, well, professionals in the art of deception as they do and say what they must to strengthen their base of supporters and appease and appeal to their constituents.

Play or engage in anything strategic and deception is lurking somewhere ready to offer you a prize, even if it is only bragging rights. A

The Development of the True Self

chess trap refers to a play that coaxes the opponent to make a move that results in their loss. In poker, players often bluff (i.e., pretending their cards hold more value than they actually do) to encourage other players to fold so that they can win the amassing pot.

In marketing, many commercials use paid actors to bring their product into our homes. And consumers almost always hone into stores that display sale signs that read *"up to a certain percentage"* or *"starting at a certain sale price."*

Even animals rely on and participate in deception. The harmless false coral snake is banded with the same colors of its venomous namesake counterpart. Eyespots that bold the back of most big cats' ears and paint the spread of many butterfly wings are said to assist in startling any predator from further pursuit. And just as these deceptions have become standard in their lineages, we too have normalized them in our own.

You see, we get so used to and so good at deceiving others that we make it far easier and less restrictive to deceive our own beings. We use it as a tactic to succeed over others, not realizing just how much we can bury ourselves in our own misconceived illusions.

And now with the internet and all the connectivity of the world around us, it is far easier for us to magnify and expand any layers of falseness. We can be bombarded with so much irrelevant and under-personalized materials and matters of the world. And then with the same technology, we can be more easily distracted, allowed, and often

ON THE JOURNEY OF JUST BEING

encouraged to be sidetracked from our own true paths.

THE NEW TECHNOLOGICAL YOU

The rewarding of falsehood takes on a new level when it comes to the ever-increasing threat of the virtual false self; all those false selves stemming from technology, social media, and the all-encapsulating internet. Technology, when we allow it, does not only replace the connection we have with each other, it can have a devastatingly undermining effect on the relationship we have with ourselves.

> **"** We have a global **CONNECT**ivity to those around the planet.

We have a global connectivity to those around the planet, but we are drastically failing at connecting to the closest spirits to us: our own being, those in the same housing, and in the surrounding community. Ironically, many of us are virtual beings, virtually being disconnected from all that we should be holding most true.

The potential to create a false you is so much easier these days and the options are limitless as the creation of such selves is often encouraged by a host of gained likes, follows, comments, and shares. It is easy for one to feel as if they are doing the right things, having the best attitude, living in their purpose, and being the best person they can be when their beliefs (authentic or otherwise) are consistently being applauded by an assortment of people, many who carry no merit to our beings, and many

The Development of the True Self

who don't even have our best interests at heart.

Furthermore, people are doing ridiculous things, changing themselves just to feel loved, worthy, and wanted. They are showering in their fifteen seconds of *"fame"* using the vastness of the internet as a medium. And instead of molding our one true being into something grander, many of us are settling or, worse, backtracking, wasting moments of a precious lifetime on a false persona or several of them. With the overuse of technology, we are attempting to find, embrace, and share our selves, while in reality so many of us are doing just the opposite.

Every now and then we must ask ourselves, would we be the same without all of these social profiles? Would we still post an item if we knew every time that no extra attention would be given? Would or could we do better? Better yet, would or could we be better? We need to ask ourselves if we are using technology to advance a greater us or are we just using it to fearfully run from it?

THE FOUR MAIN ROUTES OF PERSONAL ESCAPISM

When it comes to our authentic selves, habitual escapism can be one of our most dangerous adversaries. For how can we just be if we are consistently running away from our beings? For if just being is of position, then doesn't it make sense for us to be and move in the right positions?

With that said, there are four main routes of personal escapism, the ways in which people escape their problems as a means of trying to appease, elevate, or avoid their own lives.

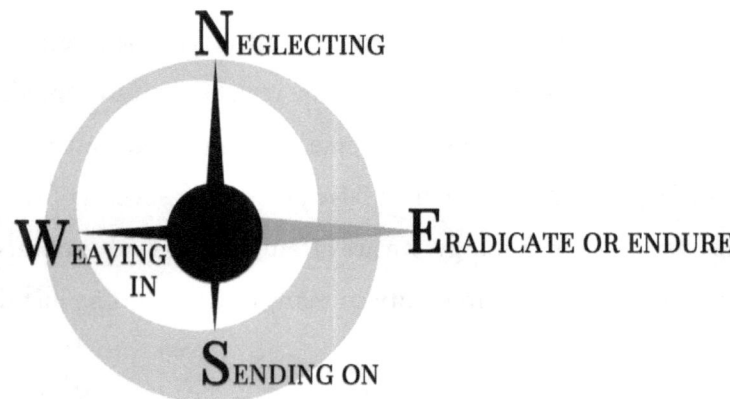

1. West, or **Weaving in Other Problems**. As a means to distract one's being from what they need to deal with, often times we explore or take on other, more familiar problems as a means to pull ourselves away from less acquainted problems or other situations that exist in our reality.

Many times, we think that if we run away from our lives, then we can protect or hide our beings from the potential dangers of the present, even though the present never really subsides. Other times we weave in other problems because we can, at least for the time being, control the conditions and our beings under them. We eat to soothe away our pains, we engage in excessive drugs and alcohol to numb ourselves so that we don't

The Development of the True Self

have to go through the coming, current, and unexpected pains of life.

Already in a state of subtle or traumatic agony, we pick the path of least resistance, and we go to where we are familiar or comfortable. But there is one major problem with this logic, and it is that most times such vices only bring temporary comfort. And if we are not actively engaged in fixing the problem at some time or another, issues often stay and may even get worse.

Trying to cure the symptoms without focusing on the causing condition is, quite frankly, a waste of time. Until we find the courage to move forward when we can, we will stay where we are in life or move directly or indirectly backward.

2. North, or **Neglecting your Problems**. These are people who ignore or try to ignore the major problems in their lives.

    Of course, all problems don't need to be addressed, and there are some problems that don't need a resolution right away. But some allow many issues to be without resolve, even when solutions are relatively simple or easier to endure than the actual problem itself.

    People who always portray and pretend to have the perfect life (not to be confused with those making the best out of their life) are often major problem neglecters. Those that find several quarrels but never have accountability or hold a fault in any of them are also plausible problem neglecters.

Again, neglecting major problems does not make them go away. In the same respect, a different or same you do not necessarily suffice for a greater you. If an issue is consistently on your mind and you are making no plans or doing nothing to get rid of it, then it is bound to stay, and it is bound to assist you in lengthening a false sense of self.

3. South, or **Sending on Their Problems**. Instead of dealing with their problems, such people willingly delegate or force them upon other individuals.

In a career environment, this may be acceptable. The CEO passes on work to the managers and the managers again to lower staff and so on. But in most cases, outside of institutions, this is unacceptable, especially when it comes to the development of our beings. And if you are the one always sending on your problems, find the courage to work through them so that you may learn ways to pass difficulties and better deal with them if they so happen to return.

On the other side of things, note that it is great to network and it is wonderful to assist. But if someone is affecting your being with issues they are not even trying to resolve themselves, then

The Development of the True Self

it may be time to cut their concerns loose! Instead of always giving them the opportunity of comfort and mediocrity, give them chances to work on handling their own issues so that the both of you may have the option of growth.

4. Lastly, we can find a way to mitigate or erase our problem's power over us by choosing to move East, to either **Eradicate or Endure the Problem.** Of course, for all obvious reasons, this is the best option. Though it will also require the most honesty, integrity, vulnerability, and courage, it will be the direction most worth it, as forward is the direction in which our character is most aptly built. For where the mind has strength, soon do our bodies and spirits. Thus, soon do our beings.

Also keep in mind, as mentioned in a few examples above, that we will have concerns that fall and move in between and amongst the most distinct points of N, E, S, and W, as most of our problems are not that easily navigated.

But in any matter, even though no critical problem or situation will be simple or without some level of agony, forward is the only way we prove and convince our minds that what seems implausible can be made, in fact, into reality. This is what keeps us going, and this is why going forward is so significant. Yes, going beyond our current situations may involve hurt, but that pain is nothing compared to the hurt involved while moving in the opposite direction, or at the very least, staying where

ON THE JOURNEY OF JUST BEING

we are when progression is readily available.

The next chapters speak on the journey of moving forward, how essential it is for growth, and how it expands our beings in a more palpable and inspiring way. Such journeys may seem sometimes treacherous, but as we will find, our beings were made to be boundless.

A journey-less life is often wasted, but a life on a journey not only explores, it is explored. It lives, it thrives, and it conquers! For when we honor our power as one, our beings take root and we, with less uncertainty, begin to grow.

On the Journey of Just Being....

SECTION 2
of Creation

Begin Become Beware
uile Betide Betroth B
ehave Befriend Besti

CHAPTER 5
Your Power as One

> *"Many of us think or portray that it is the realization of our potential that determines our significance, but, in fact, it is the realization of our significance that leads us to our potentials."*

HONORING OUR POWER AS ONE

At times, we falsely perceive ourselves to be so insignificant simply because we see ourselves as only one.

"Little ole' me, how can I change the world? For I am just one person."

Although we are indeed individually one person, as we've seen throughout history, one person is enough to bring significant contributions to the way in which we all live. Because one is closest to zero, we must not misperceive our power. For we ARE powerful and we already hold the potential willpower needed to make our lives as purposeful and as great as they were meant to be. For it has been proven time and time again that one of many things, let alone us, is enough to

ON THE JOURNEY OF JUST BEING

mold an impression into a mountain.

Do not make the mistake of devaluing the object of your being because it is only one, for one is where all grand things start. One microscopic sperm meets one microscopic egg to create one relatively giant human being. Towering trees start off as only one small seed, and all great actions start off with one intangible thought. Every hour starts off with one minute, and each minute with one second. Thus, we must understand that we are not as one where it all ends, but in contrast, we are where all mastered and amazing creation begins and continues to grow, even beyond that of our existence.

You can't have two seconds without the first one, and a tree certainly cannot grow without the unit of its makeup planted so properly in its purpose. It is our power as one that allows us to find, express, and essentially be at and within our highest potentials.

With that said, many of us think or portray that it is the realization of our potential that determines our significance, but, in fact, it is the realization of our significance that leads us to our potentials, as how can we reach any level of greater potential without first consistently being aware and implementing our known and eternal worth?

Furthermore, if we are always looking for our significance solely as a result of meeting our potential, when life throws us curveballs, we will feel as if we aren't as successful as we should've been and often find our significance seemingly tarnished. So often we depend on life to make us feel of importance instead of allowing our importance to give to us

Your Power as One

life, to make us feel and be greater than our physicality of being just one. For when we are aware of our significance we offer ourselves many opportunities to advance, as to be is to foster buds of creation, as to be is often to grow.

In addition, we must know that our utmost potential as a human being can never really be accomplished, at least in our own individual lifespan. It is a goal that has no finish line, a mountain with no peak, as our glories are very much that arbitrarily high. And for that reason, it can never be fully realized. But as awful and limiting as this may sound, this is actually a good thing. It shows us that our greatness is so magnificent that it resumes long after we're gone, that the effect of our power as one lingers for an infinite number of lifetimes in both idealistic and tangible forms.

Just because our maximum potential can't ever be realized in our lifetime doesn't mean that a higher potential should bear the same fate. And just because we are already significant doesn't necessarily mean that we are using our significance to achieve the goals of our greatest selves.

> " The irony is that many people let their **OVER**all lack of limitations be **THE LIMIT**ation.

The irony is that many people let their overall lack of limitations be the limitation, they let fear and other false senses get in the way of a greater self and then find joy in the mediocre complacency of their drive. We know that we can go far, especially when we witness others doing so, but yet some of us choose relatively not to even move.

But despite how we may feel, this life, this world, this universe is here for us. I'm not saying that it's just for you or it will be easy and always fun and filled with amusement. What I am saying is that you were made by an infinite creator, and a portion of such limitless essence lies in each and every one of us.

We are all imperfect people, to say the least. And even though we may have a body of people working for us and helping us to be, we should all embrace the embodiment and manifestation of understanding and appropriately using our power as one so that we approach our sense of being with greater ease and accuracy.

Successful people do extraordinary things not because they were or are super human, or because they have a power greater than the rest of us. They were and are extraordinary because they answered the call to be, to just be, to just be greater than their yesterdays, even in times when being who they were meant to be was difficult.

No matter how hard their lives were and are at times, think what they would've been like if such honorable people chose not to be. Think about what it would've meant for them, and then think about what it would have meant for us.

Can you even fathom that world? And this is just a handful of those who simply and rightfully used their power as one, people who were born with beings no more significant than anyone else. History may have made

Your Power as One

them known and even admired, but they were significant before history knew their name and I believe they'd known it. If they hadn't known it, I'm almost positive many wouldn't have taken the risks they did to get them to a place of such profound destiny.

They were significant before the rest of the world admitted, though often, everyone else is just slower to acknowledge the fact. As such, greatness and its associated acknowledgment will often and inevitably fill us up once we are determined and ready to embody it.

You, in your own custom-made power as one, can enjoy the mastery of being you just as any other can. And that is a gift in itself, in which life does not give you the option of being anyone else because who you are is so extraordinarily special and personally significant.

Your power as one lies in only place: you. And the secret to harnessing its graceful magnitude starts with the recognition of your authentic self. There are three major commitments one must accept, prepare, and consent to in order to authentically feel and understand their power as one. They are to (1) forgive the past self, (2) accept the present self, and (3) use the present self to prepare for the future self.

THE FORGIVENESS OF THE PAST SELF

Admit it, we've all done things that were, at the very least, absolutely stupid. We've all said some things that were ignorant, immature, or quite plainly unnecessary. We've all projected our troubles and insecurities out on people who had absolutely nothing to do with them. We've all mocked

ON THE JOURNEY OF JUST BEING

and ridiculed. We have all lied, and we've all hurt someone, intentionally or not. And just as much as we've loved someone else, we've probably hurt or traumatized our own being.

With that said, it is not a surprise that we can hold grudges toward ourselves, accepting our *"failures"* as a part of our beings. Far too often we hold onto all that we have endured, the sufferings, the financial and circumstantial difficulties, the abuse of trust, the misuse of friendship and personal space, and the self-betrayal of broken promises made to ourselves, implied or explicit.

It is important to know that these things will always be in our past, but the debilitating and the weighted remnants of them do not have to dwell within the mass of our beings in the present moment. Thus, we must not only wholeheartedly seek forgiveness from others, but we must also sincerely seek it from ourselves.

> We must not only wholeheartedly **SEEK FORGIVENESS** from others, but we must also sincerely seek it from ourselves.

From here on out, whenever we feel the past beginning to bring us down, we must declare that our present and our future self is and will be better. We must know that our past is here to teach us something(s) and we've got to hold on, not to the past itself, but to the lesson(s) it so appropriately provides.

Your Power as One

It is the past that comes to make us strong, to show us what is of love and what is not. I believe it does not occur to give us fear, melancholy, shame, or regret, as again, we willingly tend to adopt all of these things ourselves. Contrary to widespread belief, the past is here to help us, to give us reasoning and insight so that we can better map the intricacies, pitfalls, and even the joys and pleasures of our journeys. When we pay attention to what the past tells us, we make room to pass whatever it is we may be facing.

You see, life throws us into times of darkness not so that we can stay there. Sometimes, we are put in the *"darkness"* so that we can find and acknowledge new spectra and the wavelengths of light we often overlook in the brightness of all our good days.

And though it is truly impossible to live in the darkness of the past, as the past cannot be physically lived in, it is entirely possible to live with all the stuff that it brings up to the present. That is why we must not only forgive what the past has brought to the surface, we must fully acknowledge all the damage we put up with and carry on our journeys so that it can be properly discarded in the realm of the current self.

THE ACCEPTANCE OF THE PRESENT SELF

While we come to mentally grasp the concepts of our past, we too must deal with all things present. And let's face it, many times our current situations are more daunting than our pasts, because (1) it's happening right as we endure them, and (2) the lessons that erupt from our issues

ON THE JOURNEY OF JUST BEING

are not always as apparent as when looking at them retrospectively.

But do not be alarmed, here is where our power as one thrives. All the present wants you to do is accept it; all it wants you to do is accept your being and just be in it. In the past, we've been, and in the future, we will be, but only in the present can we appropriately and most naturally just be.

When we do not or cannot fathom accepting our present selves…

1. **We Won't Get to Enjoy It.** And who doesn't want to enjoy the present? After all, the cliché does proclaim it is a *gift*.

    A lot of us tend to ignore or ill-perceive the present when times are really good or when they are really bad. Don't let these extremes get to you. We can't physically live in the past, we can't physically live in the future. So, if we are not physically and mentally living in the present, then when, how, and where are we living?

2. **We Create Lousy Pasts and Lousier Futures.** When we attempt to live in the past or in the future, we void our power as one to null. Thus, as time goes on so often does the nature of our circumstances.

3. **It Will Be Harder for Us to Get Past Our Issues and Situations.** Stressing out over the present in tough times clouds our thought processes, it tires us, and it makes us less apt to conquer whatever it is we need to endure or overcome.

Thus, ignoring the present won't do us any good either, for how can we ignore something and wish to change it and make it better, even if it's already good?

4. **The Lessen Might Go Unnoticed.** If we don't acknowledge our being in real-time and the lesson is apparent, we most likely won't be able to see it until later. When we are not as attuned to what our voices are telling us, into what God has planted deep inside of us, we tend to focus on all the negative aspects of the present and the possible near future.

5. Lastly, when we do not or cannot fathom accepting our present selves, **We Often Repeat and Possibly Worsen Our Problems and Issues.** Again, we can't change it if we don't see it as true. And if we are not getting the lesson the present sometimes exposes, it is more likely that we will fall into a personal disharmony and make way for the repetition of poor results to occur. Instead, we need to be making way for our breakthrough, as just because we can't change the past doesn't mean we should recreate it in our present and future.

Furthermore, just because we have accepted our present being doesn't mean we must accept staying in the environment this being resides around and/or takes in. The present, under any circumstances, is not immune to change, so how and why can we expect or demand ourselves to remain the same within it?

ON THE JOURNEY OF JUST BEING

Yes, some things just may have to remain at least for the moment (i.e. certain illnesses, your stature or weight), but use your being to work around these variables, for these things are not all things. Accept yourself for who you are, but never settle for who you could be. Many of us want change but have yet to change the way we view ourselves. We want change, but we haven't begun to accept the body for which the change must occur in.

> " Many of us want change but have yet to change the way we view ourselves. We want change, but we haven't begun to **ACCEPT THE BODY** for which the change must occur in.

Therefore, accepting ourselves in the current moment is vital to our beings, as more often than not, we do not readily change for objects, ideas, or persons we don't accept, love, respect, or care for. For where is the logic in using or building upon what we already perceive as useless?

If we can accept ourselves in what some would call troubled times, we will be more apt to accept ourselves and be fully absorbed in those times that are good. Consequently then, we can better prepare ourselves for the magnificence that is still to come, for the being that is our future self.

THE PREPARATION FOR THE FUTURE SELF

Preparing for your future self, contrary to popular belief, does not

Your Power as One

start in the future. It starts in and within the now, as it is the now that soon becomes the future.

You don't need to start on New Year's Day, on your birthday, next month, or *"after the holidays"* to be. There is nothing more special about these days when compared to another. That's why when it comes to initiating, working hard, or accomplishing part of your being's goals, there is only one day better than the rest, and we call that day today.

With that said, before we get into a hoopla about preparing for our life journey, know that our results may not replicate exactly what we have in our minds. Our journeys are always unpredictable at best. But as unpredictable as they may be, this does not mean they are impossible or that they can't be enjoyed along the way. For as long as we have awareness, instinct, and sightedness, the present and the past will be there to guide us.

We may not always know where we want to go in life, we may not even know who we want to be yet. But we should not let that stop us from taking estimated guesses. To be honest, sometimes, we just have to rule some things out. And while we do that, we should familiarize ourselves with the trails of our past and present journeys, learning to find joy and enlightenment in our walks as our beings edge toward that of a greater destiny.

ON THE JOURNEY OF JUST BEING

If you do know what else you want from life and that of your being, then you're that much closer. Now, all you have to do is make a plan and commit to getting there. Of course, as you make way, life will come to test you. Don't be surprised, but remain optimistic as it is all just preparation for your future self and the building and holding of your power as one more effectively.

Many people are shocked and bewildered when *"life"* shows up in their lives. This is because many of us have failed to realize our power as one, and consequently so, we tend to belittle the greatness and resolve that manifest from it. But if we are growing, if we are becoming more of our true selves in each waking day, and if we are becoming stronger and more resilient in who we are as a being, we gain raw insight and encouragement in knowing that the vast majority of our hardships or our pains won't always be around, especially as we learn to conquer them.

There are some methods that have been explored and are undoubtedly here to help us forgive our past selves, become one with our current selves, and help us prepare our future selves, all the while embracing our power as one. Some of them you may be familiar with, while others you may not. I suggest you do your own independent research on them and find out which methods and/or alternatives work best for you and the coming of your greater being.

That being said, as I talk about these practices, one may associate them with a particular culture and religion. It is important to know that these are just practices. And while they may be used in your religion/

Your Power as One

culture or one different from yours, they are not solely defined by any particular sector or institution.

For instance, we all communicate, but that doesn't mean we all speak or gesture in the same manner. And this is okay, as long as we understand more deeply how we connect with each other using our thoughts and emotions proficiently. Again, communication when done effectively, holds the same outcome even when different methodologies are used. And the same perspective should be used when analyzing and implementing the following practices, all aimed to heighten our power as one.

We all convey and receive messages, not only with others but with ourselves as well. Sometimes, this is just done merely with thoughts until such is voiced through a language of dialects and accents. Other times, conjointly so, we move more than our lips as we engage in a gestural state of speech. Yet in many moments, and profoundly so, we aim so loudly to convey our words or thoughts with silence.

THE SILENT TREATMENT

Have you ever gotten so mad at someone that you used the silent treatment on them; that is, you became so silent you forced them in an odd and simplistic manner to pay more attention to you? Well, the same principle can be used inwardly, and we can use this practice to actively listen to the reclusive, drowned-out, suppressed inner voice that often evades us in our busyness.

ON THE JOURNEY OF JUST BEING

The point of the silent treatment, which is too commonly called the vow of silence, is for you to place yourself in a quiet place, remove any sound that may be of diversion, including, and perhaps more importantly, the sound of your own audible voice and force yourself to proactively listen to the inner you, to that being so normally muzzled by outside distractions.

The silent treatment is a great way to deal with the past and the present because it normally finds for us the things we'd just rather ignore. It discovers situations we thought we had resolved, but in reality, had only pushed back into our subconscious. It makes us deal with our problems, forces us to address our vulnerabilities, and also, and most importantly, it opens us up to a great space and mindset of healing.

You see, the silent treatment, as the name implies, is treatment.

The thought of so much silence may seem a little extreme and can merely sounds impractical. Honestly, it can be both. So, this is where the modification comes in. Obviously, the silent treatment needs to have a constructed time and place in your life to be successfully implemented. You can't go to your place of work and not answer phones and go to meetings having verbally isolated yourself.

To make the silent treatment work, you might want to schedule a weekend with yourself or take a good amount of time to partake in this practice where your silence does not harmfully affect anyone else. With that being said, if you don't want to face the experience alone, you too can make it into a couple's or friendship experience.

Your Power as One

I challenge you to at least try it if you haven't already. Yes, it may seem agonizing, and it may well be in the beginning. But once you dump all that dead weight, you will have a feeling of refreshment and a lightness that you've probably never felt before. For there is a good reason why the other practices often directly or indirectly require or encourage some form of silence.

Silence can soothe us during relaxation, and the void of our societies' noise within nature can bring one to a complete and all-surrounding peace. In prayer, silence offers reverence as we prioritize our focus. And while engaging in meditation, silence often delivers a powerful concentration that allows us to acknowledge our power as one during the course of passing privileged moments.

MEDITATION

Meditation is here to help with the present by making us, well… present. As a basis for meditation one is told and encouraged to breathe, an action we partake in all our lives but never stop and really think to pay attention to. It mentally slows us down and often exposes us to how we seemingly live our lives, but sometimes forget to live in the moment as greatly and as boldly as we should.

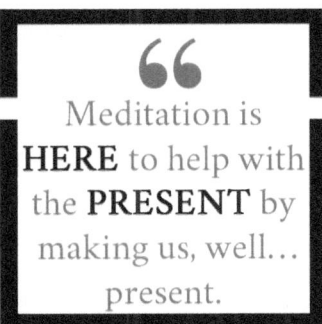

> Meditation is **HERE** to help with the **PRESENT** by making us, well… present.

It is a method that also teaches us how to quiet and organize

ON THE JOURNEY OF JUST BEING

our minds, which can be, as I'm sure you know, a battlefield of ideas, thoughts, feelings, plans, and perceptions. Overall, meditation is a great way to decrease all of this chatter and allow us to focus on the raw power of the now.

It is a way for us to create an experience with our beings like never before, for us to again practice listening to our most inner instincts and voices. In fact, the Tibetan word for meditation, *Gom*, practically means to become familiar or accustomed to one's self, to one's true voice.

You see, the object of meditation is to practice capturing yourself in the present so much until it becomes normal, acceptable, and fully encouraging for us to live there. By then living in the present, we can harbor the most extensive abilities in our choices to fervently enjoy the moment or willfully or too skillfully change it.

Another adjunction to meditation, which you may or may not implement, is called a mantra. Mantras are small sayings that are repeated during meditations to affirm whatever the being is hoping to receive from the experience or in life in general. They can be traditional mantras starting out as simple as the sound om, or you can opt to use more contemporary mantras like short or shortened scriptures from the bible or speaking into existence an inspirational life quote. Whatever you choose, if you so decide to take part, make sure that its manifestation is healthy for the soul and appropriate for your being's journey.

Again, there is a ton of additional research out there so find out what works best for you. There is also a number of apps that can be

Your Power as One

purchased or downloaded to your electronic devices to assist you with your meditation experience.

Also, keep in mind that if you don't feel that your mind is as *"quiet"* as you'd like it to be during the experience, continue to focus and don't give up. Meditation, as with anything, takes practice, and soon you will be a pro!

To meditate, all you will need is a small, quiet, comfortable space. Meditation usually lasts a few minutes and can be performed daily, or one to a few times a day/week according to one's need or preference.

PRAYER

No matter where you do it, prayer is essential for the maintenance of a sound mind. If you want assistance with the past, present, and future, then you can be sure that prayer helps. It is timely, it's humbling, which goes well to reducing the false almighty ego, and it lets us know that it is okay to ask for help. It reduces stress and stress-related illnesses, and for that reason, scientific studies have suggested that it could be a big factor in the increase of one's lifespan. So not only are many living longer lives, their quality of

>
> Prayer uses faith to **DRIVE OUT FEAR**s and anxieties that often consume and stagnate us.

ON THE JOURNEY OF JUST BEING

life is being heightened. Thus, we are more apt to reach our authentic selves and do so for more sustaining periods of time.

But prayer's greatest component is, perhaps, faith. Prayer uses faith to drive out and mitigate the irrational fears and anxieties that often consume and stagnate us.

Celebrating and enacting faith in the good that is around and within us is a key component in acknowledging the limitless potential of us being. For if you don't believe you are capable of great things, then you will tell yourself subconsciously that your being doesn't want them, and that doing anything complementary to achieving your greatest self is a waste of time. Consequently, of course, this often prohibits one from doing what they need to do to be, and be at and within their greatest.

But prayer helps to defeat this. It pushes, encourages, and lets us know that self-betterment is both wise and more importantly achievable. It relaxes us, allows us to tap into the highest being so that we can find and heighten our own unique power as one.

RELAXATION

For obvious reasons, relaxation is a great gift, though many of us don't get, use, or take part in it as much as we should, as relaxation actually allows us to enjoy and mentally take in the achievements of us being.

Instead, many of us would rather opt to take part in overstimulating entertainment, spending excessive amounts of time with technology, and idolizing our work more than our own flesh, as if we are or could be composed of it.

Many of us fear relaxation or feel as if we don't deserve to indulge in it at all. And even more feel like they just don't have the time. But ironically so, when we don't take time to relax, our moments seem to move a whole lot faster.

If you are a *"relaxation neglecter,"* let me tell you that such perceptions are often misleading. Time, yes, is important. And work too is important and should be done in a timely and appropriate manner. But if your life is all about work, you will totally miss the purpose of life and will have actually done yourself a disservice, wasting time you thought you had utilized effectively.

With that said, if you actually enjoy work and it is in an odd and beneficial way of relaxing, then you just may have found your purpose. If that is the case, such a circumstance should be recognized as a gift and should not only be practiced more but also honored.

Also, know you don't have to be plotted on someone's beach on an island far off from home to relax. Yes, distant vacations are nice, but they are not always plausible. Instead, as always, do what you can.

Yoga, Tai Chi, and other similar classes are great forms of motioned relaxation. Properly situated between the stillness of meditation and the stress-relieving modes of exercise, these subtle movements of strength, flexibility, and prowess can certainly and surprisingly be just what we need to de-stress.

ON THE JOURNEY OF JUST BEING

Other options include reading an enjoyable book, sitting down just to sip and actively enjoy some coffee or tea. You may want to close your eyes and mentally go on that vacation you've always wanted to go on, or imagine that dream that you are thinking about or working on accomplished. You may want to confide in a good friend, in a diary or journal, or perhaps even the warmth of an aromatic bath.

These are just a few examples of what you can do to relax, but of course, we couldn't forget to mention the last section of this chapter, which is to surround yourself with the vast relaxation of nature, a place where all conspires to be.

RE-ALIGNING WITH NATURE

If you know anything about me, you probably know just how much I am an advocate for people to safely and responsibly spend some time re-aligning their beings with nature in whatever ways that suit one's comfort.

Nature, as I'm sure you've witnessed, can be a marvelous place. It is a place of destiny, the sweetest and best mixture of adventure and peace. It overpowers our senses with sounds, smells, and visions and makes one willingly want to be present in it. You see, this is what is so spectacular about nature, especially when the markings of humankind, our makings and machines are not overly present. Nature is teeming with vitality, and I argue that this is, in many cases, what makes the value of nature so remarkably immeasurable.

Your Power as One

Nature is the living example of the phrase *"just be."* Trees grow without thoughts of how great it would be if they were skinned with another bark. The birds don't fuss about the changing of seasons, but instead, through migration, they readily adapt to life's seasonal shifts. The grasshoppers aren't jealous of the butterfly's wings, and the silent hills only speak volumes of tranquility. This is why the outdoors is so great. This is why we are so in tune and so attracted to it, even if it is only on the screens of our televisions.

You see, we need nature to not only remind us of our true beings but to bring out all the hidden wonders within us, to show us that the world is ours to grow and flourish in. It manifests our dreams right before our eyes, exhibiting to us how beautiful it is to just be and proving what is possible even in the harshest of conditions.

Nature is also a transforming example of just what it means to use our power as one in conjunction with other beings. It shows us just how moving our beings can be of great growth even when we aren't physically moving, as nature, in many aspects, illustrates the bold act of stillness.

CHAPTER 6
The Bold Act of Being Still

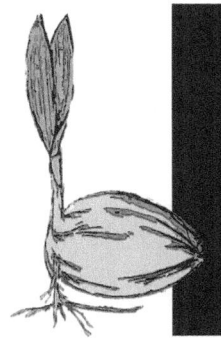

*"Stillness strengthens us
from both good and bad sides,
and it allows our beings
the chance to adapt to the endurance
required at times for our journeys."*

FIGHT *NOR* FLIGHT

When life shows us beauty, it is relatively easier for us to be still and enjoy it. But when life gets tough, we more easily fall into our evolutionary ways, and quite naturally the flight or fight response takes over our attitudes and ultimately our behaviors. In such times, many of us either try to fight life, or we desperately try to run away from it. A lot of times though, there is a resounding boldness and an immense advantage when we use our beings in the most efficient way, when we appropriately choose to just be...*still*.

As humans, we are thinkers, constructors, leaders, and creators of many mediums. Generally speaking, we can pave portions of our life to lead us ultimately where we want to go. But true to our nature, we have the will and the determination to want to control everything, including the totality of life itself! Of course, this is not remotely possible, but it doesn't stop us from trying anyway.

But just think about what would, and what does happen to us when we never think for once when the times are right, stop our vehicles at life's stop signs, yields, and stop lights to really focus and see the potential hazards or the beautiful scenery instead of always just driving right past them. Imagine if we didn't pause to redirect our routes in better times and to better directions, or cease our motions and emotions to fill up our fuel tanks. Imagine the wear and tear and the two inevitable conclusions of a constant heightened level of drive, as we'd either (1) break down, or worse, (2) crash.

> " Imagine if we didn't pause to re**DIRECT** our **ROUTES** in better times and **TO BETTER** directions.

So you see, being still at its worst is not all that bad. It gives us a chance to slow down, to really be cognizant of our beings and the present that it dwells in. It allows us to properly discern why we are in a good place or predicament and more proficiently, what we can do to change it if we so desire.

In addition, stillness strengthens us from both good and bad sides, and it allows our beings the chance to adapt to the endurance required at times for our journeys. It lets us see the reality of patience and the

The Bold Act of Being Still

benefits it can offer. It provides inspiration and motivation and tests our discipline, showing us often why our demanding work is necessary. And in a lot of ways, it humbles us, getting rid of those egos and stopping us from thinking that we can live our lives alone.

There are three main instances when being still is appropriate: when we cannot control our overall circumstances, when we can conserve and use our energies more efficiently, and to make the good times even better than they actually are.

Once we are able to be still with those persons and circumstances that require us to be, we are able to see life in a different light, and we are able to use, redirect, and conserve such energy that is often unnecessarily exhausted in our intent to flee or fight.

FIGHTING LIFE

So often in life, we unnecessarily carry with us the heavy armor that we've convinced ourselves that we need for whatever circumstances life has dealt or is dealing us. And we go to war with certain circumstances before realizing we don't even have to.

Trying times are not strangers to us. Life, of course, will not always be as nice and as easy as we'd like it to be. But often, instead of utilizing the unique abilities and remedies of stillness, in the midst of our troubles, we begin the exhausting and useless process of fighting life.

We put our beings in battles trying to change people, attempting to turn back or speed up time, and trying to skip the journey just to get to the destination. Sometimes, we fight the life around us not because we want to go to war but because we know no other way to survive. And sometimes we fight the life within us not because life's battles are desired but because we just don't know how to be still. For even in storms can peace lie, that in the center of every hurricane is an eye of serenity, that in every thunderstorm is the calming effect of raindrops spliced with the roaring music of thunder.

So often, we take fighting the aspects of life—you know, illnesses and diseases, negative habits, strained relationships, and even our purposes—and somehow begin to equate the experiences of fighting life itself with combating our own being's existence. We take fighting portions of death and turn them, willingly or not, into fighting the very premise of our greatness.

With that said, being still does not mean we must give up and allow our conditions to consume us. On the contrary, it means that our beings must be conscious enough to know that we are not the totality of our problems, that our problems do not have to define our beings or the life that they've structured, that our battles with ourselves don't always have to escalate to wars.

> **❝**
> Those that swim with life's current know when to **BE STILL** and when to swim.

So, if we want to know whether we are fighting life or being still when life finds it appropriate, here is how we may differentiate the two.

The Bold Act of Being Still

Overall, those that swim with life's current know when to be still and when to swim. While those that fight life almost always swim against the current, as those that fight life often...

1. **Try to Change or Control the Current Without Changing the Current.** They don't change or control themselves properly in the moments they inhabit. Of course, in life, this cannot always be done in haste, and sometimes it can't be done at all. But so many of us try or at least want to change their problems without even acknowledging their place within them.

2. **Find Themselves Always Exhausted with the Same Problems and with Little to No Progress.** We sometimes spend most of our time swimming upstream, staying in the same place or going in the wrong direction instead of embracing the journey and using that energy into becoming better beings.

3. **Fight and swim against the current of life because we Are Either Focused on the Past or Because We Are Afraid to Move into the Future.** We stay in the same place because at that moment we are fearful, trying to figure out every aspect or solution to our concerns. Also, sometimes, we are afraid that if we let go we may never comprehend or accurately analyze our current situation. But the truth is, sometimes, there just isn't an explanation. And more times, at least part of

the answer one seeks waits for us downstream of our path.

Many times, we don't want to move into the future because we think or know that the future means more hurt and more sorrow, as if staying in the same place isn't going to create the same or worse results. We cannot believe what has happened to us and so we wonder and prematurely disapprove what life has in store for us. We imagine our own destiny and see it as if it was not made for our beings to thrive in it.

4. **Wish to Move on or Change, But Instead, Find Steady Position Hanging onto the Wrong Emotions.** We grasp onto bitterness, anger, denial, depression, jealousy, and grief like they are rafts, when really, they are rocks. And grief as not only defined by the consequences of physical death but also the deaths of relationships and old habits. And while we can totally understand why one will and should feel the need to grieve, we should also understand that we can grieve *and* move forward in the current that is us being.

Overall, it is also wise to understand that in each case fighting life leads to one or two things: wasted time and/or wasted energy. But the great thing about energy is that it can be manipulated to our advantage. Biological (living) energy can be transformed into chemical energy and equated into metabolic energy to bring us the energy we need to survive. Chemical energy can even be converted into light, which is the process

The Bold Act of Being Still

deep sea creatures and fireflies use. They use energy to their benefit and so can we!

You see, flowing against or with the current is really about how we choose to manage our energy, whether we exhaust it uselessly or use it for and within the confines of our purpose.

We all carry a curiosity or passion inside of us, a fire of gifts, of a career, or close relationships and we get to choose how to use that power. Either we will use that fire to tear down and wreak havoc on our lives, or we can use it as a light to guide us in the now, as warmth to defrost our hearts when we feel it growing cold. Either we will choose to be immensely sorrowful in our losses, or we can live remembering all of the good times we've once shared. Either we can choose to be angered at what life has brought to us, or we can use that same energy to truly make our lives and beings better.

When we appropriately move downstream, we can more easily progress, and we don't have to swim nearly as hard to find our greater selves. Yes, there will be boulders rising from our rivers, and there will be rapids from time to time. We will have to swim and redirect our courses, expending wanted energy for good purposes many times in our lives. But that doesn't mean we meaninglessly swim upstream, that doesn't mean we are to attempt to stay in the same spot when life is always pushing us in the direction of our destiny and purpose.

Every year, an uncountable number of salmon in the North Pacific travel upstream and quite literally fight for their lives in the quest to

ON THE JOURNEY OF JUST BEING

make new portions of it. None to few of them make it back to the sea from which they came.

During the same year, a greater number of birds take to the skies for their bi-annual migration, and like the salmon's experience, it is an arduous journey. But the birds have become experts in what it means to just *"go with the flow"* of life.

At times when the weather and winds are unfavorable to the direction in which they want to go, they pause their travel. And instead of flying inexhaustibly in the tall skies, they remain relatively still on the textured ground. There, they feed and rest and gain the energy they would have otherwise wasted. They know they can't control the wind, but as soon as the winds turn to move in their favor, they take to the skies and use the aerial currents to take them where they need to go.

They would undoubtedly meet the same fate as most of the salmon if they'd ever decided to purposely and consistently go against the wind in any other way than needing the lift required to get them off the ground.

Similarly, our lives are and were not made to be more difficult than we sometimes make them. Sometimes, all we really have to do is just be still and go with the flow. Problems will arise as they always do, but the more problems we face traveling downstream, the better apt we become at flowing right pass them.

Thus, many times it is okay to be still and just let life take us on the amazing journey that is the betterment of our beings, and to preserve such a splendor in doing so, to simply be by resting.

The Bold Act of Being Still

REST

    Another time we must be still is when we truly feel we have no energy left, or more proactively, when we use rest to maintain and conserve energy to further perpetuate our being's productivity.

    We are all familiar with the heart's beat *"lub-dub, lub-dub."* But what many of us don't know is that when the heart gets into one phase of its rhythm, the heart does a remarkable thing. The cardiac muscles relax, the valves drop, and the heart fills up with what it intends to circulate. You see, roughly 50% of the time our hearts are working, and the other half of the time our hearts are resting; our hearts are being still.

    Our brains too need rest much the same. They function superbly when we are well-rested. But as soon as we start to become sleep-deprived, our bodies start to feel the effects (i.e. loss of focus, irritability) of not finding a sense of inactivity. Go twenty-four hours without sleep, and the brain automatically sends us into a mild state of madness and delirium.

    With all of this noted, if our two most significant organs need rest to thrive, you'd think that would make for a convincing argument as to why our beings need it also. If our sustaining hearts and conscious-giving brains need repose, you'd think more people would find rest and thrust it to the level of significance that it deserves.

    Instead, there are many people who see rest as a sign of weakness or as a waste of time. Ironically so, weakness cannot even be properly analyzed if we are not alert enough to gauge it and time cannot be wasted

ON THE JOURNEY OF JUST BEING

if we are not around to use it.

Every year, nearly 1/3 of Americans admit to dozing off behind the wheel, not only putting other lives in danger but their own too. If that isn't literally a wake-up call to get the rest our body and beings naturally demand, then I don't know what is.

We should remove this connotation out of our society that perceives appropriate amounts of rest as a bad thing; that if one needs rest they are automatically lazy and often so inadequately and prematurely prone to ill judgment. For your bodies command rest for many reasons.

When we have rest, it does wonders for us, and when we are lacking it, we can put our beings and those of others at risk. In addition to accidents at the wheel and other accidents, including those that are work-related, chronic sleep deprivation (and even mild sleep deprivation in some of these instances) can negatively affect your:

- Memory, increasing lapses of memory and the creation of false memories
- Cognitive activity and attention to detail
- Libido (sexual drive)
- Fertility
- Mentality, and may cause and be linked to depression and anxiety, even hallucinations and mania

The Bold Act of Being Still

- Weight loss, as the lack of sleep stimulates the hunger-stimulating hormones
- Judgment, much like mild amounts of alcohol does
- Alertness, and our ability to gauge it
- Aging and cosmetic appearance. They don't call it beauty sleep for nothing
- Mood
- Personal and professional relationships
- Agility and reaction time
- Stress hormones
- Awareness
- Healing and the ability to grow
- Overall feeling, as the lack of sleep can induce or exacerbate malaise.
- Immunity
- Vision
- Body temperature
- Exercising and muscle strength
- Empathy and the other perceptions of people's emotions
- Tolerance to pain

- Attraction to the opposite sex, making you attracted to those you may not otherwise be attracted to
- Creativity
- Planning and coordination
- Ability to control habits
- Ability to act appropriately under pressure
- Energy levels and endurance
- Risk taking, causing you to take more risks than what is ordinarily appropriate
- Brain cells
- Speech
- Patience, and
- Problem-solving

And with all of the above symptoms, it is no surprise that sleep deprivation has also been linked to a number of illnesses, conditions, and diseases. These include:

- Inflammation
- Confusion
- Sleep paralysis
- Attention Deficit Disorder (ADD) and other similar behaviors of hyperactivity

The Bold Act of Being Still

- Dizziness and fainting
- Upset stomach and nausea
- Sore muscles
- Hernia and muscular fascial tears caused by the overexertion of impaired muscles
- Fibromyalgia
- Osteoporosis
- High blood pressure
- Arrhythmias (irregular heartbeat)
- Heart disease or heart failure
- Type 2 diabetes
- Cancer
- Seizures, and
- Strokes

Sleep deprivation has been realized to be so devastating that, unfortunately, it is and has been used literally as a ploy of torture. If this is the case, then why do so many of us willingly torture our own being? Instead of a self-inflicted disparity, why can't we just find the time, the will to sometimes just be...still?

With that said, it is understood that many times, for a period, a significant amount of rest is just unavoidable, as I'm sure new parents and

ON THE JOURNEY OF JUST BEING

a host of students can attest. The thing is that we don't get used to not getting an adequate amount of rest or use typical stimulants as a constant replacement for sleep.

If you are having problems sleeping, I urge you to see your physician or a sleep clinician to know what you can do to enhance and better your sleep and rest experiences, as a plethora of benefits come with proper rest.

Rest makes us healthier, more alert, and more productive in both our thoughts and working procedures. The less stress we go through in our lives, the more our bodies are better apt to adequately heal, prevent and inhibit stressors, strengthening our beings to greater capacities. Rest and sleep will put us in better moods. Not only are we more likely to live a longer life, but we are also more likely to be fulfilled in the life we're living.

> **REST** makes us healthier, more alert, and more productive.

You see, by being still when times find it appropriate, we are able to bring more into our lives by doing less. Even when times are great, we can get more from our experiences by being still, distant from any distractions. By engaging and focusing on the present moments, by unplugging and decluttering, and continuously being here with our beings, we gain the ability to make such moments more enjoyable.

UNPLUG AND DECLUTTER

The Bold Act of Being Still

Decluttering or simplification is not about being perfect or having a boring, tone-deaf, colorless life. Simplification is essentially about getting rid of all the unnecessary electronic and organic noise that surrounds and blocks our life's melodious song in all the times we should be singing it. It is about getting us to the point where we can hear our voices, identify them, acknowledge them, and most importantly, learn to love them if we haven't already. Decluttering allows us to shape our environment as best as we possibly can. It allows us to actively soak in some of the best moments of our lives as we more easily flow down the rivers and streams to greater destinies.

Somehow, many of us have misunderstood this concept of simplification. Just because we have complex minds and can build complex items and create complex things, many of us have been convinced that our lives, too, have to always be immersed in a state of complexity. And this is just not the case. Thus, many times, in our efforts to make our lives more *"interesting"*, we only seem to make them more complicated, sometimes unfortunately so, more complicated than what we can handle at the given moment. If at times we are to just be and in these moments be still, it is imperative that we fully understand the purpose and art of simplification so that we are able to be still in some gaining or gained motion of clarity.

If life is like a river and at times the best thing we should do is to just flow with its current (as opposed to fighting it of course), the more complications the river faces, the harder it will be for us to move on. And if our water's flow is fully obstructed, we may even be diverted from the path we so wish to travel.

Overall, it seems that if we ever want to make something better, more has to be added onto it. Our beings have to be overly layered, our closets have to be fuller, and our minds littered. But most of the time, the more we decorate our beings with needless entities, the more we begin to lose facets of our genuineness.

Simplification, however, removes, prevents, and lessens the dams that we or others build in our lives so that we may be, and be more comfortable living out our destined trajectories. Simplification pushes us into authenticity, and the more time we spend with ourselves, the more familiar we will be with our beings. With that said, keep in mind that sometimes others are put into our lives to cause dams. Such people re-route our course for betterment and put us on or back on our most appropriate journey.

In addition, we must understand that our lives cannot and will not be simple all the time, as both routine and unexpected challenges regularly occur. Luckily for us, a little stimulation from a challenge is a good thing. But this doesn't mean we should go out of our way to make

> **SIMPLIFICATION**, however, re**MOVES**, prevents, and lessens the dams that we or others build in **OUR LIVES**.

The Bold Act of Being Still

our lives more complicated than they already have to be, especially for non-progressive reasons.

But even in our difficulties, we can learn something, even if that something is to actually learn to steer clear of clutter and unnecessary distractions.

There are two main components in people and things that clutter and prevent us from getting to the state that is just being and just being still. They are (1) people and things that waste our time more than they add value to it, and (2) people and things that waste our energy more than they supply it, and they often work together to cloud the path of our movements.

When you invite or encounter life's clutter, it will undoubtedly attempt to dam your flow. It will be the hoarded boxes crowding around the space of your being, it will be the gales of wind that try to push you off course, and these are the most common ways they tend to show up:

1. **Useless Relationships.** When we feel we can't properly be still in our own currents, it can be relatively easier to get caught up in someone else's. As a result, we end up swimming in the direction of their flow, their purposes, and often their misguidance, wasting valuable time and energy, all the while wondering why we haven't achieved all that we've wanted.

   If you are going to be or are sharing a considerable amount of time with someone, make sure their streams are flowing in a similar direction and speed as your own. Make sure their currents flow freely with yours. Otherwise, you'll just end up being taken for a ride.

2. **Useless Jobs/Careers.** If you are not passionate or at least intrigued by your daily duties and are not working toward fulfilling the potential of your being, then guess where you will be? That's right, stuck between and behind a flow that is not even yours.

   A job should ideally be a partnership. The business/company should be giving you something (in addition to money) in exchange for all that you are providing (in addition to your time). You may be gaining money, lots of it, but over time frustrations and resentment may come as you become more aware of valuable time and energy that could have been used much the same elsewhere.

3. **Living in the Future and the Past.** Again, you can think about them, but so many people try to live in them and this is not possible! Beat-up torn boxes from the past litter people's rooms. Unmarked, unopened, and unidentified boxes block the hallways, windows, and doors just the same, sometimes seemingly providing no route of real escape.

With that said, when we can only spend time in the present, why allow ourselves to essentially be trapped outside of its current?

Why do we fall into this trap of unnecessarily overcomplicating our

The Bold Act of Being Still

lives? Here are a few reasons.

1. **Fear.** We complicate our lives because we feel it is easier to hide in them than to be free in its vastness, especially when we feel we don't have the confidence to muster the responsibility of such freedom. We fear failure and surround ourselves with useless relationships because sometimes it's just so much easier fostering, maintaining, and dismissing beings other than the levels of our own. We fear the present by blaming the past and remaining faithless about the future. And not only do we fear the being that is us, we, many times, fear the work that is required to get us to where and who we need to be.

   We must know, and as we will further see, that real relationships with real people require real work, even and especially when that relationship is with ourselves.

2. **Ignorance.** Sometimes people just don't know. That is one of the many reasons why I wrote this book. I wanted others to know because when we know better, we become more aware and we, at least, give ourselves the opportunity to improve.

3. **Distractions.** We are marvelous beings with multifaceted minds, but sometimes our greatest asset can be our worst enemy, as we are so easily distracted. We stick one toe in another person's stream, and before we know it, we are neck-deep half a mile away from where we were.

ON THE JOURNEY OF JUST BEING

We are curious, often distracted by love or numb by heartbreak. We are beings that like to be engaged, and in many aspects, this has taken us far. But awfully in so many ways, it has also taken us far from ourselves, which leads us into the second portion of this section: Unplugging.

We are so busy trying to get the latest editions in style and technology that we forget or neglect to purchase, upload, and install the latest and fixed versions of ourselves. We can't go 2 seconds without a phone but won't spend 5 minutes trying to actively sort out and mitigate all of the drama and overcomplexities in our lives.

> **"**
> Purchase, **UPLOAD**, and install the latest and fixed versions of ourselves.

If we are not using such technology in a way that strengthens us, instead of just as a status symbol, or a fix to fill some type of void, our boredom, and/or our needs for gaining excessive amounts of attention, then just how much is such innovation really serving us? Then can it really be labeled by our beings as an innovation?

Here, in this new-aged technological world, I fear many of us are starting to believe that we are made more of 1's and 0's than the DNA used to carry the potential greatness of our humanity, the greatness in finding emotions, creating thoughts, and building relationships in which a technological device cannot. Many of us are unwittingly and

The Bold Act of Being Still

without care disrupting the relationships we have with our beings, and consequentially so, are disrupting the relationship we have with others, with some of the most important people in our lives.

The next chapter highlights to us how our beings affect those around us and how those around us, conversely, can affect our beings. To be is to grow, and to be together is supposed to aid in growing us closer. As our companionship toward each other develops and individuals push relationships to their greatest heights, those in the given relationship consequently are forced to push themselves to that of their greater self and that of their conjoined sense of being.

CHAPTER 7
Being in Relationships

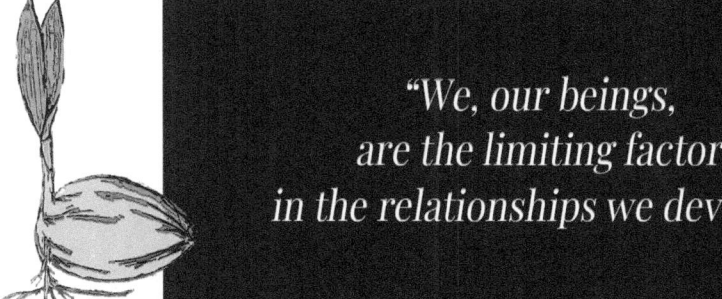

"We, our beings, are the limiting factor in the relationships we develop."

THE MIRRORING OF BEINGS

Most likely, you will have close relationships with your children, your parents, your spouse, and close friends. But by far, the most personal relationship you will ever have with any human being will undoubtedly be the one you foster with yourself.

With that said, know that it is perfectly acceptable to spend alone time with yourself every now and then. You could and should go to the movies, to shops, and out to dinner with yourself from time to time, especially if you are single. Know that it is perfectly acceptable to dance and have a song that symbolizes all the promises of adoration you have for yourself. We must know and be aware that there is a stark difference

ON THE JOURNEY OF JUST BEING

between being lonely and being alone. And if you don't want to be left alone with yourself, it would be ironic to think of and complain if others think the same way.

Do not consistently feed yourself the narrative that *"I only matter when"* or *"I am not enough until"* I am complimented by someone else, as we must remember our power as one and its ability to grow ourselves apart from a partner or another.

It is important to stress this point because, in general, unless you have a strong relationship with yourself, all other relationships you participate in will suffer in some aspect or another. Because we, our beings, are the limiting factor in the relationships we develop. We determine how our relationships are built, structured, managed, manipulated, and ended. We are the living example of how others should treat us, and we consistently provide a fundamental example of how others think they should be treating themselves.

We often set the tone for others' behaviors aimed in our direction. And the purpose of our connections, good or bad, are often the glue underlying each of our bonds, acting as a mirror between parties to show us our own clear or blemished reflections.

> " We often **SET THE TONE** for others' behaviors aimed in our direction.

If you're a raging bull, yes, some will run, but other raging bulls will stay just to coax the whistling steam from your nostrils. If you are a poisonous snake, only other

Being in Relationships

poisonous snakes will be able to withstand your presence for extended periods of time. If you are a butterfly, you will seek the same flowers as other butterflies that float among that gentle breeze. Lions will pride and wolves will pack, and if you are a timid mouse, you will surround yourself with other mice so that your appearance may be diminished and your sense of security increased.

No, we won't and cannot totally be the same, but generally speaking, the relationships we tend to harbor share strong similarities. Go ahead and ask yourself what characteristics bond you and your closest of friends. You see, relationships, especially when we are molding our beings, are used to attract and assimilate us to both ourselves and those in part who share our preferences.

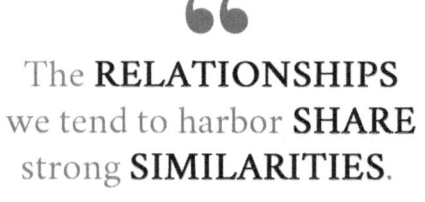

> The **RELATIONSHIPS** we tend to harbor **SHARE** strong **SIMILARITIES**.

Children always seem to be inadvertently taught guidelines for relationships by observing and imitating the relationships around them. The same can be said in dating and other relational scenarios involving significant others, as it is definitely common for others, even those who claim to love us dearly, to treat us how we tend to treat ourselves.

You see, when you love yourself unconditionally, you open yourself up to unconditional love. Because you are familiar with it, it becomes more easily recognizable. You will be able to see it and, most of all, you will be able to properly receive and use it to fill you up graciously as

ON THE JOURNEY OF JUST BEING

it comes. Also, when you love yourself unconditionally you can give such energy more easily onto others. And with a love that strong, you undoubtedly have the power to positively affect the world around us.

In contrast, when we surround and willingly take parts in unhealthy relationships, the love our beings deserve and feel is diminished, and the feelings our beings sense show themselves in a seemingly devaluation of their character and consequently in that of such regarded stemming expectations.

THE DEVALUATION OF BAD RELATIONSHIPS

Relationships have the potential to hold magnificent value. However, not all relationships we find ourselves in are beneficial, as some actually devalue our beings all the way back into varied unauthentic levels of falsehood.

As mentioned before, human beings, just as a hoard of other animals (i.e. birds, antelope, and wolves), seek out relationships not only for pleasure and companionship but also for additional safety. However, many times, this primal instinct to seek company is stronger than our desire to actually pause, acknowledge, and take action for needed concern. And instead of giving portions of life as good relationships do, bad relationships corrode the very premise of our existence. It causes confusion and consequently devalues the all too vital relationships we have with ourselves and others close to us.

So why do we find ourselves in love with people who cannot or

Being in Relationships

choose not to reciprocate the adoration given? Well, there are several reasons. But often, we devalue our beings by defining, unknowingly or knowingly, our relationships with:

1. **Compensation.** As we grow, we sense the feeling that we lack a portion or portions of ourselves and so we look to others to fill them. We want to feel as if someone loves us, we want to cure our loneliness, and solve the mystery of our emptiness. We want to feel good and so what better way to do so than to accept another person into our lives, as we assume that, perhaps, they can feel the voids we seemingly can't.

2. **Skewed Views of Ownership.** No, not exactly in relation to slavery but rather in a way that tells us that something *"belongs"* to us and that we have the seemingly great privilege to *"belong"* to someone else.

3. **Boosts of Ego.** It is the immense feeling that one gets, not because one has a lover, but almost solely because that person is there. But as we've seen, the ego can be as blinding, if not more blinding than *"love"* itself. Just because someone is with you and it feels good doesn't mean that they are with you for good reasons. Just because someone is with you for the moment doesn't mean they'll be with you aside from that season. Just because someone seems to love you more than you do yourself doesn't mean you have to grow arrogant of this love and not build up your own wealth of confidence. For

there is a certain humbleness in what is true love, and its grace overpowers all that is of our ego.

4. **Abuse of Power.** Relationships can be a direct link to a greater sense of power. There is power in knowing that you can make someone angry or happy, power in knowing that you could will someone into giving portions of their mind and body to you, and power in knowing that you have some control in some area or aspect of your own life and those that you attract to associate with it.

5. **Validation.** Relationships, when created, no matter what form they come in, can cause one to feel as if they now matter. We think that when a bond is created, however appropriate or timely, its creation is always indicative of our beings at their greatest holding it together. People get caught up thinking that the relationship is sustaining itself when the bond in the relationship is actually being sustained and supported more so by sex, money, time, or attention.

And of course, the dangers of validation always persist when such confirmation and the permission to be and be without is needed. That is, if your being only matters when someone else is around, what happens to it if they leave, cheat, or pass away? That is why the totality of your worth, again, should never be completely dependent on someone else's presence.

Being in Relationships

6. **Concealment of Self.** Sometimes, it's just easier to focus on someone else's life than it is to focus on our own. We often try to hide our beings behind others, intending to replace fear with *"love"*. But depending on the people we invite into our lives, we might just be adding company to our misery.

7. **Biology**. As mentioned before, there is an innate urge for us to seek companionship. A host of chemical reactions and biological responses play out as we touch, feel, and sense what we come to know as attraction, lust, love, and adoration.

   Biology, too, as you can see, has its motives. And it is quite frankly not exactly to love…but rather to have us procreate, which is not at all to be confused with us having sex for pleasure. Sexual activity doesn't feel good for us just because… in the same way nectar isn't sweet just because flowers want to hold something inside other than water.

   Fortunately, time has thankfully led our beings to favor life. If sexual activity wasn't as pleasurable for us as it is and has been, then there would certainly be less of a powerful incentive for us wanting to or circumstantially continuing our species.

8. Lastly, **Excitement.** Relationships, especially new relationships, can be terribly exciting, especially when combined with our biological drives. We all like new things, even if, and perhaps, especially if they are people.

ON THE JOURNEY OF JUST BEING

With all of this said, no relationship or beings within them will be perfect. Mistakes will be made and apologies, when due, are hopefully given. But the key to finding and maintaining a successful relationship is finding and keeping someone who encourages you to be and be greater, and for you to do the same for them, even if it means the both of you will ultimately be better apart.

> " The key to finding and maintaining a successful relationship is finding and keeping someone who encourages you to **BE** and be **GREATER**.

In the greatest relationships, you are free to be, and you are encouraged to heighten this being. There is no need for falseness, no need for ego, and no need for shame or pretenses. Your life partners should not only want you to be because they love you, but also because they truly enjoy the company of your being.

This, again, is why individualism needs to be sought after just as fiercely as social likeness, even in relationships, and perhaps, especially in times of deceit or betrayal.

Not surprisingly so, many people that have been hurt, in true mirroring form, grow quickly to reciprocate the feeling. Though most times we are able to grow more and pass such situations when we just allow ourselves to be, when we are able to think consciously enough to ignore the natural law of received emotions when it comes to irrelevant negativity.

Being in Relationships

REVENGE, RESENTMENT, AND THE NATURAL LAW OF RECEIVED EMOTIONS

Each profound relationship will have some moments of instability, and many will not echo the traditional hoped-for fairy-tale ending. For those that don't, it is imperative that one tries their best not to fall victim to the casualties of hurt, for there is no way of hurting someone and also not damaging yourself in the process.

Just think about it: If you punch someone, your knuckles will bruise and bleed, the same way a car wrecks if it collides with a barrier or another vehicle. This is Newton's third law of motion converted sagely into the natural law of received emotions, that when one body exerts a force on a second body, the second body simultaneously exerts a force equal in magnitude toward that of the first body. It says that when it comes to our emotions, for every action, there is an equal opposing reaction.

> ❝
> Revenge and resentment are just as, or more self-afflicting than, their **ATTEMPT**s **TO** reciprocate the hurt **RECEIVE**d.

And while the hurt may come from another, revenge and resentment are just as, or more self-afflicting than, their attempts to reciprocate the hurt received, as they, unfortunately, tend to keep us reliving our troubles over and over again.

ON THE JOURNEY OF JUST BEING

Revenge and resentment are the relationship epitome of unnecessary cluttering. They often make themselves apparent in useless or tiresome relationships, both are rooted in fear, and both involve that person tying themselves tightly to a negative past. Overall, they are a big waste of time and energy.

And not only do they block our course of desired destinations, they also keep us on the very same course alongside those or those actions we are probably not too fond of. We are so quick to hate someone for all the wrongs they do or did to us, but often and without accountability, we go and spread the same vile that we found disruptive to our beings. And because we must embody malevolence before we can spread it, when we do dish it out, our beings and those we hold still close are often the ones who continue to receive the most anguish.

Sometimes we pull ourselves so far from our own beings that we cannot even identify where all the hate we possess comes from. Then soon we frequently have to face the long journey back to ourselves amid the longings, betrayal, and all the turmoil of heartache.

Many times, we feel our apologies are unwarranted, or we don't know exactly how to give the necessary level of kindness to both the agitator and ourselves. But still, even in these times when anger urges you to lose yourself, it is best to just be and stay found.

Yes, you may still be sad; yes, you might be hurt, but at least you won't be all of these things in addition to not being you. Furthermore, I know a lot of times we turn to revenge and resentment, not particularly

Being in Relationships

because of what others have done to us but just because we allowed them to do it.

Sometimes we somewhat willingly leave our beings in hopes that revenge and resentment find us a bolder version of ourselves, but this rarely happens. Honestly, the strongest thing your being can do is to successfully go through (and not live with) all the feelings of hurt, shame, and possible guilt. To be vulnerable with ourselves, again, is not an indication of weakness, but on the contrary, it comes to show us just how strong we can be when we really need the strength.

But too, keep in mind that you don't necessarily have to express anger or sadness to be resentful and seek revenge. Sometimes we keep our composure and try to hurt the receiving party in a different aspect by showing them in some way or another what they are or have been missing, if indeed they have been missing anything.

And because our motives are indecent even though our attitude *appears* to be positive, the natural law of received emotions still applies and we still run the risk of wasting time and energy, as such valuable resources could be used for actually doing something more productive.

And the more we participate in the subtler forms of revenge and resentment, the more we tend to leave our confidence and esteem with not only another person, but with another person who may not even care about our happiness. We must ask ourselves: If they are really as bad as we often portray them to be, then why would they even care about what kind of success I achieve?

ON THE JOURNEY OF JUST BEING

And when we do find *"success"*, considering our attempts to make another look or feel bad, chances are we would have come into a greater success, a more sustained longevity of it, and/or a greater sense of ownership toward ourselves if only we had been working on our truest being and not toward the detriment of someone else's.

So many of us want to *"teach"* our betrayers a lesson, but quite often in doing so, our attentions are so outwardly focused that we begin to disregard the lessons that we are supposedly teaching. And in many ways when we exhaustively and purposelessly try to *"fix"* another, our beings begin to degrade from our own persisting neglect.

The stark truth is that many times when we engage in revenge and resentment in the context of a relationship, what we are really doing is subconsciously continuing the relationship, whether we truly want to or not, even if it's a bad one For if we really hated someone so much, I'm thoroughly convinced that we'd try our hardest to distance ourselves from them as much as possible.

But all too often we fear being alone with our troubles. We fear that things won't be as good as they once were, and in fear of also being wrong, we sometimes do whatever it takes to make the feeling of being right a continuing realization, no matter how wrong, in actuality, this may be. Overall, it's not the presence of hurt that brings us the most grief; it's the betrayal. It is the lack of love.

You see, no matter how it is expressed, all revenge and resentment really are is a longing for love, and this is why and how the subconscious

Being in Relationships

relationship is continued within them. This is why revenge and resentment are so devastatingly corroding to those who embody and amplify it.

And that is why in such times of resentment, we need to long for and obtain the necessary love that we have seeded within, the love planted in us by our creator, and easily grown with our will and discretion. And in such times of revenge, we are to tighten our relationship with God, as from this connection draws to and from us more love, unconditional love—a love like that of water that flows to and washes over every crevice of need.

Instead of repeatedly getting hurt seeking something to go wrong for another, we should be getting better at seeking something to go right for us all. For there is no greater mirror than love and no better resounding growth than that of spirituality, as such allows us to be greater by giving our beings ever-permitted access to that of the greatest. For here is where greatness is. For here is where we are ultimately and most purposefully destined to be.

On the Journey of Just Being...

SECTION 3
of Greatness & Positive Influence

CHAPTER 8
Being Spiritual

> *"Just being becomes a lot more effortless when we are able to share our space and burdens with the one who shows all the aspects of love."*

REACHING YOUR GREATEST SELF

By now you may be wondering, when it comes to your greatest self, how do you know if, in fact, you are experiencing or have experienced it? And to be honest, there is no one straightforward way to answer this.

Your greatest self may be difficult to define because there is no one universal equation to get to it. There is no one grand action to conjure it, no specific time or time of day one holds it. It can be as quick as a passing smile or as long as our hours of noble service.

Your greatest self has neither age limits nor age requirements. And while it can be influenced by others, it is not solely dependent on them. Often immersed in one's dreams, your greatest being is beyond

ON THE JOURNEY OF JUST BEING

description, and because its origin and route can be highly mysterious and even abrupt, it is sometimes not as apparent as we'd like it to be.

But one thing is certain, once one has reached their greatest self, they won't have to question their aptitude of being, as they will experience oneness with the world around them. They will encounter themselves being so well that they will be in sync with their own destiny and in all the ways it sustains them.

But most of all, as with all things personally and profoundly deep, reaching our greatest selves is nothing short of a spiritual experience.

> **REACH**ing our greatest selves is nothing short of a spiritual experience.

With that said, so often we confuse being great with having great things. As a result, we often make our talents larger and hold our blessings higher than the beings that are ultimately designed to contain and maintain their excellence. We sometimes get lost in our own popularity and pride because those around us choose to love our talents and traits more than the essence of our own beings. And many times, in such environments, we convince ourselves to do the same. We think of ourselves being magnified solely because everything else around us is.

But you don't have to be the most attractive, the most talented, or the greatest person of all time to be at your greatest. All you have to do is consistently and authentically be.

Being Spiritual

With that said, if you're wondering if, in fact, you are reaching your greatest self, here are a few indicators: True love will be surrounding, peace will embolden you to a sense of security, happiness will overflow from you, and your acts of service will fill not only your being but also the multitudes of humankind.

Remember that to be is to be positively influential alongside a state of confident greatness. And as our creator influences us in great ways are we able to do the same onto others both nearby and afar.

This chapter is about embracing all of these characteristics so that we not only gain the level of greatness our authentic beings desire, but to begin to acknowledge and understand just why spirituality is key to the preservation of our beings.

WHY SPIRITUALITY IS KEY

Where religion is based mainly on a set of practices (i.e. prayer, communion, meditation), spirituality is what brings meaning to these practices. And while religion is mostly physical, spirituality, as the name implies, is something greater. It provides the context and reverence needed to truly believe, and it gives us a greater discernment to better understand the complexities of our beings. Metaphorically speaking, if religion is the package, then spirituality is what is inside; it is the food that acts to sustain us.

With that said, we have people that hold strong to religion, but their packages encase little to nothing. And we have subsidiaries of religions that spoil the food, severing their connection to greatness, while also allowing others to throw a false blame on the totality of religion and sometimes spirituality itself. Then again, we have some religions and subsidiaries of such that do well to foster and keep fresh our spiritual substances.

Thus, proper spirituality grants to us faith and exemplifies what it means to reach out, connect, and bind to something larger. It acts as a conduit for manifesting the greatest parts of ourselves, which then allows us to be at our greatest.

Spirituality is the connection that unites us to our maker. It is the fullest expression of our essence, as we are aware and appreciate the very life force that allows us to be. It is often directly unheard or unseen, but it is almost always greatly felt. And when demonstrated properly, spirituality allows for the presence of our portion of God to show itself and fill us up from within. Fundamentally speaking, spirituality is the conscious acknowledgment, acceptance, and sharing of God's love.

And as simple as that sounds, such acceptance sustains us while we're being and encourages us to not only love this being but others as well. True to righteous spirituality, it does all that God's love does. It strengthens us when we are weak, moves us when we are stagnant, balances us while we are reaching for heights of

Being Spiritual

greatness, and humbles us when such pinnacles are conquered.

This is why spirituality is such an important component to our authentic selves and to that our greatest beings. Besides, how can we tap into our greatest selves without tapping into the greatest portion of ourselves, the part where God resides in all beautiful and grand splendor?

UNLOCKING THE GOD IN YOU

You may not be perfect; you may not be the greatest person in the world, but the greatest entity that has ever driven energy into this world and outward lives, in part, in you.

We must know this! And more importantly, we must feel this! We must know that we share the same forces that span across boundaries we have not yet traveled. That when we were created God deemed it necessary to place a portion of such power within us, for us to cherish and hold dear.

With spirituality lying in the middle of our ethereal selves and that of our physical beings, we have a direct link to the creator of our entirety and yet many times we willingly miss or dismiss the feeling of God's overpowering presence. But why exactly is this?

1. **Our Egos Are Too Big.** A lot of times we confuse accessing God with trying to be or thinking that we are the totality of God. But only when we are humble do we allow room for God's love to fill us. For when we are *"full of ourselves"*, it leaves no room for the expression of God's bounteous magnificence.

ON THE JOURNEY OF JUST BEING

Just being becomes a lot more effortless when we are able to share our space and burdens with the one who shows all the aspects of love. When we allow God to carry what we can't, like for instance the massive weight of our egos, we are able to get to a greater place in life with less energy expended. And as a result, we can shift more energy toward making our experiences even greater, as such energy that can be utilized to move our being forward into betterment.

2. **Bad Times.** Many times, especially in those despairing or discouraging times, we may feel that God has left our side, even in circumstances where we knowingly neglect our own beings and consequently cut off the living God that nurtures from within. Other times, it is easier to blame God than to take responsibility, give attention to, or change the cause that created the situation in the first place.

    Sometimes and oddly enough, God puts us in such situations so that we may have the opportunity to see his grace more clearly, to allow and urge us to be, and to also analyze and process what the world is like when a loving God isn't collectively expressed through the spirit and goodwill of our beings.

3. **We Fail to Believe.** It is hard to reach that fiber of us that connects us to the almighty when we have no urge to believe.

Being Spiritual

We isolate ourselves and then wonder why we don't feel God's presence, as if all connections don't require at least two points and a bond somewhere planted between their beings. And in general, how does any relationship survive when one doesn't believe in it?

We believe in the invisible forces of a gravity that may weigh us down and wind that could, under extreme measures, blow us away. But somehow, when it comes to the lightness of God's love, we, even believers, especially in tough times, have periods of doubt.

Lack of proof is what many will contest, but I argue that the proof is quite evident because the creator of life lives in all of us. So, if we really need proof, it would benefit us more to stop looking for it solely outside of ourselves and start searching for God's love more so within. Where there, God's mercy and love is all the proof of God's profound existence we'll ever need.

4. **We Don't Know Ourselves as Much as We May Think.** As such, many of us fail to consistently witness the grandness of God within us because we have yet to realize the grandness of our own beings. We don't find it plausible that something so amazing could enter us and reside because we have not seen our beings and their potentials as deserving, as worthy. But we

ON THE JOURNEY OF JUST BEING

are.

Just think, if we can't come close to ascertaining the fundamental depths of ourselves, how can we even begin to truly comprehend the complex, extraordinary, and infinite being that is the portion of God that calls our being home?

When we find spirituality, we find the ability to believe, to humble ourselves, to see the good in troubled times, and to find ourselves at greater levels of proficiency. It is here in spiritually that God has allowed us to bear witness at our discretion and encounter his priceless and uncountable works, not only to be worked but worked from the very depths of our own true and gracious spirits.

> When we find spirituality, we find the ability to **BELIEVE**.

Knowing that we are enough, and finding and growing the peace, happiness, and love that lives within us are all spiritual acts. They connect and grant us access to the greatest parts of our creator and, thus, allow us to reach the greatest parts of our being with more ease.

YOU ARE ENOUGH

It is spirituality, the acknowledgment, acceptance, and sharing of God's love that tell us beyond the shyest doubt that we are enough!

This is one of the hardest concepts for us to understand en route

Being Spiritual

to our greatest selves. Sometimes, what we don't see and feel persuade us into believing lies of self-incompetence. As a result, we often feel we cannot do or provide progress to our goals and beings, and this just isn't true.

Because we all walk around missing something in our lives (i.e. love, loved ones, money, our definition of success, or our dream careers), we sometimes tend to think that we are (1) not enough, (2) not good enough, or (3) not enough to be. And again, such notions couldn't be further from the truth!

You.

Are.

Enough.

You have a portion of God in you, how can you not be enough?

Many of us get discouraged by the puzzle of life, but really, it is how you view this puzzle that helps to determine how well you can reach modules of your greatest self and how long you are able to then sustain them. For when it comes to life or aspects of it, there are 4 types of puzzlers:

1. The **All-Piece Puzzler**, they, because of ego, ignorance, or the fear of gaining more pieces, think for sure that they have all or most of the pieces to the puzzle that is life.

   They've managed to fit some of the pieces together, and because they see a small vision of who they are or who they want to be, they falsely think they've gotten the full picture.

ON THE JOURNEY OF JUST BEING

Notice that this section is called: *"You are Enough"* and not *"You are (or have) Everything."* God is the only entity that is and holds everything. Luckily for us, we share a part of God, and because of that, we are automatically provided with enough.

And because the All-Piece Puzzler feels they have most or all the pieces, they naturally lack both the will and intent to look for more.

So, what can this type of puzzler teach us?

- We should never presume that all the pieces are present, as we should not think of ourselves as perfect.

- Just as we shouldn't take the pieces of life we do have for granted, we shouldn't take for granted the pieces of life that haven't been given to or discovered by us.

- As we live, we can be greater in some aspect or another. Thus, we should not allow fear and ego to limit what our beings have access to when there are so many other prized pieces to be gotten.

We have enough, and the good thing is that you don't need all the pieces to see and recognize the picture. Duly, just because we

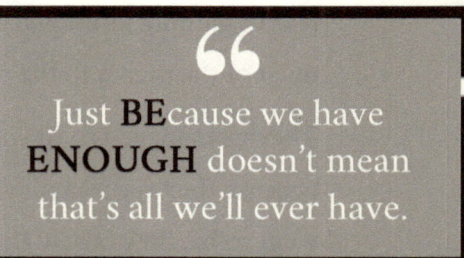

> Just **BE**cause we have **ENOUGH** doesn't mean that's all we'll ever have.

Being Spiritual

have *"enough"* doesn't mean we shouldn't be non-excessively reaching for more. Just because we have enough doesn't mean that's all we'll ever have.

2. The **Piece Collector** collects pieces that they hope will fit, that look great, and that go with what they think their puzzle will look like in the end. And for the most part, this is a good thing, as we want to collect pieces to expand our beings to their greatest capacity. But here is where many of us go wrong, and it does, of course, happen most often when we feel as if we aren't enough.

When we feel we aren't enough, we tend to overcompensate and start collecting pieces that don't even remotely belong. We hoard pieces hoping that somehow our chances of figuring out the picture to our puzzle will increase. And we accumulate more pieces illogically for the same reason a person who wants to win a raffle buys more tickets.

But as we know with puzzles, the more pieces we have, the harder the puzzle becomes to solve. Throw in pieces from other puzzles, pieces of drama, or cluttering, and you may well end up piecing a whole different puzzle altogether.

And while the Piece Collector has will, because of their lack of vision, they often lack intent. When determining what pieces we ought to be collecting, we should ask ourselves the

ON THE JOURNEY OF JUST BEING

3 most fundamental questions of being: *Who am I not? Who am I? And who do I want to be?* These questions will ultimately focus our consciousnesses so that we can narrow our decisions.

> **"** We have the **POWER** to create what our puzzles are going to look like.

But here is what we can learn:

- We have the power to create what our puzzles are going to look like. Yes, as life is defaulted, it will tend to throw in a few extra pieces, but we can add, take away, and in the end ultimately decide what our puzzles will picture.

3. The **All-or-Nothing Puzzler** is the person who notices that they are missing significant pieces in some aspect(s) of their lives and instead of trying to better complete the puzzle, they give up on attaining some of the greatest parts of their selves. They opt out before they can see the fuller, more surrounding beautiful bountifulness of their life's puzzle.

A half a pound today isn't the 30 pounds they'd hope to lose in total, so why try again tomorrow or even at all? The entrepreneur doesn't know exactly how their plan will work, so initially or eventually, they fail at trying or stop their

Being Spiritual

attempts with none to few good reasons to support their decision.

The All-or-Nothing Puzzler, because they know what they want from life, often has intent, but lacks the will necessary to bring such wishes to fruition.

But let's face it. We all fall into this trap sometime or another. In fact, it's quite natural. Time is so valuable that we tend to not want to waste it, especially when we feel or talk ourselves into seeing the outcome as unsuccessful. Sometimes, we subconsciously fear what will happen if we lose those 30 pounds or if our business plan turns out to be an enormous success.

But here is what we can learn:

- We cannot let the fear of not having all the pieces of our life's puzzle stop us from believing that the pieces we don't have are not worth seeking, as analyzing and organizing all of life's pieces offer to us patience.

- We must train our minds to believe in our due comings so that when they do come, we are mentally prepared for them...so that when we do see the piece, we will know exactly where or where not to place it. The more we work on our puzzles, the more we familiarize ourselves with them, the more we will know the colors of it, the patterns,

ON THE JOURNEY OF JUST BEING

and the shapes of our interlocking present and missing pieces.

- We must stop worrying about (not to be confused with stop seeking) our missing pieces. Such torment often distracts us from what is present and what is usable.

- We must see each piece of life as a piece of the puzzle, as a single transitional unit used to get us from one place of destiny to the next. We must use the portions of life we have to get to the pieces of life we're missing. You see, the puzzle cannot near completion without structure and purpose, and the missing, unconnected pieces are useless without an accurate and steady place of attachment.

4. Lastly, the **Master Puzzler** of life knows that they will never have all the pieces of the puzzle. Some will go missing, extra pieces won't fit, and some pieces will never be found. But it doesn't stop them from gaining and connecting the pieces they can, it doesn't stop them from capturing the essences and the beauty of their life as best as they can perceive it. The Master Puzzler fosters both intent and will and more often gets to embrace the awe of their connecting masterpiece.

While such life's solvers and master be'ers understand that their puzzle will never be complete, they also know that most pieces come with four sides for attachments, and all of them

Being Spiritual

have at least two. They know that they can circumvent the missing pieces by using other pieces to go around them as they push through voids and insecurities. And because their puzzle is nearer to completion, even with a few missing pieces, they can better sense the vision of their beings. They can properly conceptualize who they are and who they wish to be as their minds and their faith fill in the missing blanks.

The master puzzler admittedly does not know everything about life, but instead of walking around empty or baffled, they tend to carry the notions of wonder and curiosity. Instead of fear deterring them from the unknown, they tend to carry with them the longing to discover.

Thus, it is the master puzzler that attracts into their lives a greater sense of being and a better quality of peace, happiness, and love.

OBTAINING A PIECE OF PEACE, HAPPINESS, AND LOVE

There is a common misconception that happiness, love, and peace only come from our surroundings. And that if we'd ever want a chance to

> There is **A COMMON** misconception that happiness, love, and **PEACE** only come from our surroundings.

ON THE JOURNEY OF JUST BEING

hold a piece of such magic inside of us, our situation or environment must always match how we'd like to feel.

Sometimes we go as far as subconsciously waiting for our surroundings to change before we give ourselves permission to find the spiritual mindset we need to move forward. We think that if we just do *"this,"* or if we just do *"that,"* then our most desired aspects of life will come to us without any or much effort from our being. But all too often, all that this brings is a series of disappointments and eventually an overwhelming feeling of hopelessness. For it is not solely what we do, but more so who we are while such actions are motioned.

Now, I am not saying one shouldn't seek a change in environment when able, when it is potentially and positively helpful. What I am saying is that the aptitude for holding our greatest being should not always be dependent on our physical location. It is important to know that the greatest measures of peace, love, and happiness live not externally but deep inside of our beings, in the place where the core of our spirituality dwells.

Yes, your environment does help, but it doesn't always guarantee a sound mind. Only you can do that; only you can *be* that.

We all have seen people living in what most of us would call the best of environments with comparably the worst levels of peace, love, and happiness known to humanity. In contrast, we've seen many people in much worst conditions with a tremendous amount of these treasures, often holding them up in a great and misunderstood poise.

Being Spiritual

Let us now clear up this mystery. Let us know that peace, love, and happiness are here in us all, and we can learn to create and share them in 8 different ways:

1. **Acknowledge That Peace, Love, and Happiness are Here and Can Be Present.** Unbelievably, many people choose not to acknowledge that they have the power to manifest peace, happiness, and love apart from another or another environment. No, it doesn't guarantee total euphoria, but it does help one in finding supplementary peace, happiness, and love, and making them all a little easier to acquire afterward.

   So, after reading this paragraph, take a few seconds and close your eyes. Then take a few deep breaths and know that peace exists. While you're at it, smile to know that happiness exists. Afterward, find a mirror and gaze at it intensely to know that love is always nearby. And better yet, know that it was you, your soul that created these marvels just by, well, being.

   > Smile to know that **HAPPINESS EXISTS**

   Such is the physical affecting positively the mental, as our bodies link, interpret, and bring such messages into the light of spiritual truth.

2. **Find What Brings You the Most Peace, Happiness, and Love and Continually Connect with It.** Keep in mind that

this should be a healthy act (meaning it doesn't interfere with your behavior, your being, and other beings in a negative way). Take time to choose and record 3 plausible and readily accessible actions (in terms of time and finance) that you can do to instantly bring you back to a place of being at peace, happiness, and love. Keep this list on your desk at work, on your computer's desktop, on the fridge at home, or wherever you find stress is meeting you in great capacity.

Also, note that if you can't readily find one of the three, begin to look for the others. Love, happiness, and peace are spiritually linked to each other and when you can raise one, it is easier to automatically elevate the others along with it.

3. **Find the Gray Areas.** When trying to find peace, happiness, and love throughout the course of our lives, we are sometimes so self-blinded by our troubles and situations that we, too, take all the good things from our visions.

So, in times when total peace, happiness, and love is not plausible, we must healthily muster some minuscule amount of them and then learn to cultivate them into greater measurements. For it is the silver linings of life that let us know that the brightest lights are often just past the struggles of our circumstances.

4. **Practice Acts of Peace, Happiness, and Love Even When**

Being Spiritual

They Aren't Relatively or Necessarily Needed. At times, when life is good, don't abandon these practices. Become so familiar with them that you seek and acknowledge them even when it's not on purpose. Immerse yourself so much in peace, happiness, and love so that when you do need a sense of security or enjoyment you won't have to do much or exude much to get it, when then all you'll have to do is just be.

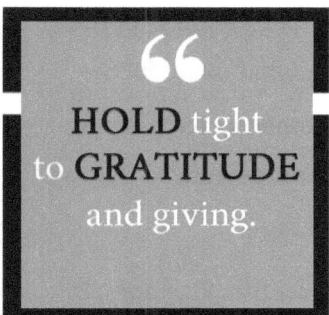
> HOLD tight to GRATITUDE and giving.

One way to continually absorb all three is to hold tight to gratitude and giving. Add a section of accomplishments to your vision board, or count your blessings literally in a blessings jar, a jar housing notes of all the things you are grateful for.

The more mindful we are of our privileges and our fortunes (however high or low we make them to be), the more conscious we will become of things that bring peace, happiness, and love to us in real time.

Giving works alongside gratitude, as it allows us to physically show our thankfulness and spread such accolades onto others. In addition, it allows us to experience the more positive side of the natural law of received emotions, as making others feel worthwhile is just as rewarding on the receiver's end.

ON THE JOURNEY OF JUST BEING

5. **Know That Peace, Happiness, and Love Sometimes Means to Lose.** We all go around with this notion that in order to gain such bounties we must gain something else to bring it to and into our lives (i.e. new clothes, a new partner, or more money).

   But sometimes we must unplug and declutter. Sometimes we must push our fears behind us and put our awareness in the forefront. Sometimes we must engage in what could be the most difficult, removing something or someone partially or totally from our lives for any given amount of time so that we and they can achieve a greater state of being.

6. **Dream Bigger.** If you are bogged down by life, lift yourself. We can use our dreams as ladders to pull us out of our miseries and into our greater destinies.

   Dreaming bigger (followed closely by doing greater) is what is going to show us that what is now is not always here to stay, that our current situation will not always be current. When we dream bigger, we begin to live in our purposes, and soon find the gained peace, happiness, and love from all the new purposes that begin to live bountifully within us.

7. When in doubt, take a few seconds to **Realize That Everything Is Going to Be All Right.** Knowing this alone brings forth soon a palpable amount of peace, happiness, and

Being Spiritual

love.

If you are going through a tough time and you've survived the moments before, then you must be aware that you have what it takes to survive the moments afterward. One must find the power in knowing that they have what it takes, that they are enough even when all emotions and others tell them differently.

8. Lastly, **Think of Peace, Happiness, and Love as Catalysts.** So often we think that one must do something spectacular and then, as a result, these prizes come (i.e. we get a new job, we buy a new car, we find the love of our life), but rarely do we put peace, happiness, and love at the beginning of the equation.

Surely, we got the new job because a confident peace was expressed during the interview. Most likely, happiness helped to steer us in the choosing of a new car. And I think it is safe to say that for most of us, some form of love was or will be present when we discover and befriend our significant other(s).

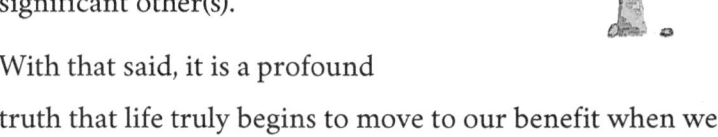

With that said, it is a profound truth that life truly begins to move to our benefit when we

ON THE JOURNEY OF JUST BEING

view peace, happiness, and love as not only good consequences but also as great catalysts, as a way to bring us into greater ways of truthfully loving ourselves and others, and having that love be properly reciprocated in happiness and peace.

With that said, many assume that the world's problems will be achieved solely by cultivating all places with an external peace. But it is illogical to sustain a peaceful world without peaceful people in it, without those happy or loved to greatly influence the landscape. It is even more illogical to bring about a world of peaceful people without having those acknowledge the authentic inner peace, happiness, and love that often lie dormant just under the coating of our falsehoods, often just beneath the misconceptions of our ill-feelings.

Though such energies of peace, happiness, and love transcend our embodiment of it, soon affecting those around or connected to us. It overflows the way nature's vast peace moves onlookers without seemingly doing much more than just being.

When we are truly enveloped in tranquility and love and happiness, we cannot hold onto all of its magnificence. And in many ways, we spread this calmed joy even in times where and when it's unintentional.

No, our problems will never be completely avoided. No matter how many issues we anticipate, get rid of, or learn to live with, more will inevitably come. But when we allow peace, happiness, and love to live within us, we start to devalue our problems instead of our beings, we start to convert our difficulties even if for a moment, from issues and

Being Spiritual

situations to *"just things"* or *"just a part of life"* as we push ourselves to move beyond them.

For to be enveloped in authentic peace, happiness, and love is to feel one with the world. It is to discover, personify, and speak directly to one's destiny as we find our way through our lives, which can be at times so thrillingly illogical. These spiritual dimensions are so powerful that they often expose to us our greater purposes in life and often give us the courage and will that allow us to go through with their implementation.

CHAPTER 9
Being of Purpose

> *"Once your mind realizes that there is undoubtedly no better feeling than the one you get giving back and doing good, our purposes suddenly become real."*

THE PURPOSE OF OUR PURPOSES

Spirituality reveals to us God's love. God's love provides to us the capacity to love, and our love often gifts to us our purpose. This is how our purposes and our spirituality are jointed. This is how we find and grow our greatest selves, how we learn to more greatly co-create our destinies for the better.

Because of this link, we tend to see our purposes in a divine light, and because they often encapsulate our destiny and explain somewhat why we have a space in this life, it is certainly appropriate that they are personally revered.

That is why, many times when we are starting to search for our purposes, we tend to look for them in their largest magnitude. We get so perplexed as to why we cannot see, or see all or most of something so *"big."* Thus, often, as we search for the purposes in our lives, we are either (1) overwhelmed by them, our search, or our findings or, (2) feel our purposes are so complex that we cannot grasp the very concept of them, even if such a concept is relatively simple.

So yes, we can ask ourselves why God put us on this earth, but there is a simpler question, a question that corresponds to another side to purpose; the side that allows us to act right before our created destinies, the side that invites us all to just be in our life's current and future intentions.

Instead of solely asking God and yourself why you are here, also ask God and yourself *"How can I use my being to best serve?"*, since to serve is the main purpose of our purposes. Yes, to be is to be great, but it is also to be of good influence, and what better way to be of good influence than to be at the service of humankind and the planet that sustains us?

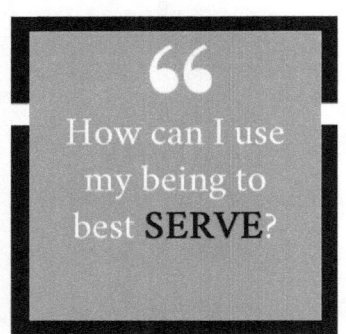

This simple question does many things, as it helps to bring all the facets of true purpose together: God, the self, and the self's service. And not only that, it brings our destinies out from the distance and right in front of our developing beings. When we begin to ask how we can be of service in the present, we instantly begin to be that of purpose and we

Being of Purpose

immediately begin to grow right into our greater identities.

Instead of only asking God or yourself what the purpose of the totality of your life is, begin to also ask what is the purpose of your life in this season. How can you serve in this granted period of time? What is the purpose of you being right now in this timely collection of moments? Is it to love even when you don't feel amply loved? Is it to find and maintain your authentic being? Is it building up your levels of confidence, or actively listen to your child(ren) when they speak?

So often we get so focused on the grand scheme of our purposes that we neglect the goals and dreams of the now. We get caught up in the unknown future, not realizing that we cannot more fully discover the purposes of our tomorrows until the purposes of our todays are realized and have begun to be worked on.

When our purposes live within our present moments, we are able to see them more clearly and we also are able to focus more on their implementation. In addition, it helps us to manage our many purposes in life, as all of us realistically have been put on this earth to embody more than one purpose, as we serve more than one body of persons or missions. Just in a single day alone our purposes can blend or shift from lovers to planners, to workers, to providers—just to name a few.

Though, when we can acknowledge and put actions to our beings in the best ways of service, we are, in turn, living out at the very least a segment of our purpose. As growth occurs, these segments begin to accumulate over time and suddenly, we are more capable of seeing and better understanding the intricate schematics of our life's purpose. And not only that, because we have already handled certain aspects of our purpose(s), many new components that come to us will be a lot less daunting than they would have been before.

For when we are engaging in our purpose's service, we are using our authentic beings to best serve by extending our greatest selves outward and onto the world. Thus, when we find ourselves both doing and being, we often find our journeys' purpose(s), as both doing and being are the main components to the equation of what is often seen as one of our lives' greatest mysteries.

THE EQUATIONS OF PURPOSE

As mentioned in the first chapter, being is essentially both a noun and a verb, and when it comes to our purposes, being definitively emphasizes the duality.

When you put both the being and the doing together for the benefit of your greater self and also for that of others, you start to cultivate and achieve your greater purposes with more ease. Thus, the principal equation of purpose is relatively simple:

(Doing + Being) = Purpose

That is,

(Serving) + (Truth, Position, Growth, Greatness, and Influence) = Purpose

Being of Purpose

You see, if you want to discover your purpose, then one thing you have to do is just be, as how can you be who you are meant to be without first being? With such in mind, here are some other things you should know when examining this equation and putting it to the use of your greater self.

1. You can just do and you can just be. But **In Order to Have and Maintain Purpose, You Need to Be Both Doing and Being.** There are so many just doing and not being and wondering why they have not met their purpose. And then there are those who are solely just being but have failed to have their purposes become a realization because they are not putting in the work needed to achieve them.

    And just to be clear, it does require some level of doing to just be, but this *"work"* is recognized as energy parading directly toward the self; it is not directly related to you being yourself so that you can benefit those around while serving in your own greatest capacity, which, of course, is often the arbitrary measure of purpose.

2. One must also note that **You Can Add and Subtract on Both Sides of the Equation.** For example, if you've wondered why your purpose isn't as productive or clear as it once was, then chances are you aren't doing and/or being as much as you were before. The amount of doing and being ultimately affects the magnitude of the attainment of your purpose at any given

period of time.

($\uparrow$ Doing + Being) = $\uparrow$Purpose

(Doing + $\uparrow$ Being) = $\uparrow$Purpose

Similarly,

($\downarrow$ Doing + Being) = $\downarrow$Purpose

(Doing + $\downarrow$ Being) = $\downarrow$Purpose

Of course, everything is relative and dependent on factors that weigh heavily on your capacity to both be and do. But whatever the circumstance, at least you will have a fundamental explanation as to what is going on, and you can better expand in ways to increase the productivity and clarity of your purpose.

3. In addition, it is important to know that **This Equation Can Be Reversed.** Sometimes it is the enlightenment of one's purpose in life that causes them to better be and do, to make their purposes greater than they were before.

    Purpose $\leftrightarrow$ (Being + Doing)

4. Lastly, as it is a means of reassurance, **It Is Critical to Acknowledge and Understand the Cycle of Purpose and Being.** This cycle allows us to recognize if we have indeed at least partially found our true purposes in the context of us being.

Being of Purpose

The cycle is simple and says to us that when we have truly touched our purpose, we naturally add energy that can be used by us to both do and be. As a result of our being and/or our doing increasing, we then add value to our purpose as the self-sustaining cycle repeats itself again.

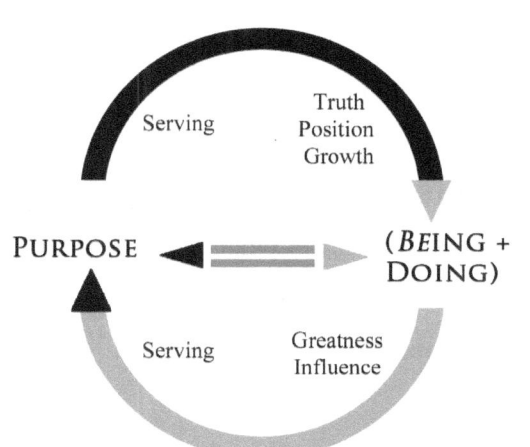

Thus, if your purpose isn't bringing you more toward your truest being, and if your truest being isn't bringing you more toward your purpose(s) AND you are being fully aware and present as to what your consciousness is telling you, your purpose at that moment probably isn't what you thought it was.

Ironically, sometimes our purpose in any particular moment is, in fact, to come to the realization that just because an action or idea is great doesn't mean that it is or should continue to be our purpose. And though this realization may not feel particularly good at the time it comes to thought, we can be wiser and better at knowing that most times the wrong purpose is worse than having and dealing with our *"little"* perceived purposes, as just because we are moving doesn't necessarily

ON THE JOURNEY OF JUST BEING

mean we are moving in all the right directions.

Also, keep in mind that doing is still part of the equation, as one cannot properly serve without, well, serving. Doing is what keeps this cycle spinning and this linear equation oscillating. It is what allows us to be within our greatest purposes and fundamentally fulfilled as best as we possibly can regardless of our circumstance.

By now, I'm sure you've got a promising idea of what it means to be, but it would be wise to also discuss some components of doing, especially when it comes to that of our beings and their dynamic purposes.

THE PROPONENTS OF DOING

Here's a quick general list of what it means to do in the context of just being.

1. **Do with Intent.** Live out your being's purpose... on purpose. If you make to-do lists (and actually use them), then you've probably figured this part out. Having plans and a strategy around them keeps us focused and on the right track, while having intent holds us accountable to ourselves and others.

   When we do with intent, we have a better understanding of our logic and the faults in our mistakes when we make them. Thus now, not only are we walking, but we're learning how to walk more properly and when and where to walk on our journeys. And while doing just for the heck of it often is a waste of time, doing with intent builds up our awareness and

Being of Purpose

consciousness. It allows us to be and live firmly and sound in advance and obtainment of our greater selves.

2. **Do with Passion.** All our passions aren't necessarily meant to be our purposes, but all of our purposes should be met fiercely with passion (or at least bold interest)! When times get hard (and yes, they will be at many points difficult), this is what is going to drive you past your situations. And not only do our passions and interests fuel us, they also act as a conduit for us to eagerly connect with those of similar or supplementary goals or those that may need our great services.

3. **Do Good.** While being is mostly for you, doing, in regard to our purposes, should be used as a platform to position you to do good onto others.

> When you are **GENUINE**ly serving others and **PURPOSE** is implemented, then there will be little room or need for greed or ego.

When you are genuinely serving others and purpose is implemented, then there will be little room or need for greed or ego. Once your mind realizes that there is undoubtedly no better feeling than the one you get giving back and doing good, our purposes suddenly become real. No longer are they just actions but

ON THE JOURNEY OF JUST BEING

now they are a living breathing organism. There is a sense of life that gleams back at you in gratification, even when you hadn't had a proper glimpse of its gaze. It is the gift you get when doing good, the gift that fills up others and yourself, sometimes in unexpected ways that keep us encouraged.

4. **Do Lawfully.** Life has a way of steering us in the direction we wish to go. With that said, we must be aware of the ways and routes in which we tread, and the possible consequences that may inhabit them.

5. **Do What You Can When Possible.** We are humans, so there will always be some limit as to what we can do, but again, don't let the thought of us not being able to do everything stop us from doing something. And if we are truly being of purpose, there will always be something to do. Plan accordingly and make it both easier for you to do and just be.

6. And **When You Can't Do, Delegate.** You won't be able to do everything concerning your purposes. It just isn't humanly possible. Whatever you can't do, find, hire, or trade off with someone who can competently complete the tasks you seek rendered.

You see, being, when combined with doing, is most definitely propulsive. But when purpose comes to fruition, our lives really begin to move full-speed. The rest of this chapter is dedicated to getting us

Being of Purpose

confidently to our purposes. It will include what we need to know, and what we will need to do to make what we know most applicable. This will include us being guided not only by our similarities but also by our differences, all the while training our thought processes to confidently know that our beings, without a doubt, matter.

BEING GUIDED INTO OUR PURPOSES

You are already here, you are already living. What more do you need to be validated?

The problem with repetitive validation occurs when people do things, anything, repeatedly just to get it, just to show others they can do something, and to show themselves that it, whatever it is, can be done. But just because you can do something, even if you are good at it, doesn't exactly mean your purpose is being fulfilled.

Please do not be confused when it comes to the differences between guidance and validation, as one is often thoroughly needed and the other is often overused. Furthermore, people often get so much more passionate about undue validation than they do for their assumed purposes when their purposes certainly have more to offer than that of unnecessary gained attention.

So, when it comes to us being in and for our purposes, why do we rely so much on validation anyway?

Well, I believe validation at an early age is vital and quite normal to our social development as the *"look what I did/made"* is then often prized by the individual as they analyze their level of autonomy and independence. In contrast, traditional notions of guidance at an immature age is often translated to and interpreted as *"you don't think I can do it/I already know how to do it."* And while validation may act as the easiest and most gratifying way of learning and building up our confidences, as we grow up, validation can do more harm than we could ever imagine or expect.

Many people are just downright fooled by how validation makes us feel. When we receive validation, we feel good, as if we've done right. And often when we don't get it, we may, well, feel all the ways opposite. Though in either case, the frequency and magnitude of the validation have much less to do with our authentic being or the purposes for which they construct.

That's why as young adults and adults, when it comes to our beings, we must begin to look more toward guidance rather than validation. And instead of assuming that the two are the same, we must know that they have their differences.

Here is how to tell them apart and why one should know more surely why guidance is often best for us being. We can better differentiate the two using the acronym DOTS:

1. **Direction.** Validation can lead us in several directions, many times, directly from our own beings. Guidance, though, better helps to steer us closer to where we need to be, toward greatness and toward that of our purposes and goals, and that

Being of Purpose

of positive influence.

2. **Origins.** While guidance comes from our *"guides,"* validation can come from anyone. They do not even need to have a real concern for our beings or their journeys. Guidance, on the other hand, when it comes to our beings, is not self-serving, but rather customized for our purposes, as it aims to serve and grow us into our destinies of ultimately being beneficial to others.

3. **Timing.** If you have noticed, when one seeks guidance, they almost always seek it before or during the activity. After all, what good is a guide after the leg of the journey has been completed? Those that look for validation normally do so after the activity or path has been realized.

4. **Seeks.** Lastly, the two can be distinguished by what one truly seeks. Guidance obviously seeks to guide, to seek the truth and purpose of our beings. Validation's purpose is to seek approval or attention.

With that said, many circumstances, including those at work, can show approval and validation to be a good thing. But validation is utterly useless when defining the totality of our being. Our creator has already approved you to be and to have a purpose, and no other human being can ever come close to God's firm and resolute authority.

Now that we have a better idea of guidance and validation, and the effects they may have, let us discuss the greatest variants of validation. (1) The urge to matter, the validation to others that you are or can contribute to society, and (2) the urge to be different, the validation to others that you can contribute to society in a way no one is currently doing and/or in a way no one has ever done before.

YOU ALREADY MATTER

The more we try to convince others that we matter, that we are loved and cherished, the more we inevitably end up trying to convince ourselves the same. The more we feed ourselves this notion of *"I just don't matter,"* the more we will believe in this falsification and the more we will crave such validation, continuing the tragic cycle until we, or perhaps someone else, genuinely realizes our unconditional worth.

I see it all the time—the need for people waiting for someone to realize their worth, sharing their good experiences solely because they must rely on the reactions of others to determine their past or current successes, or how they should feel about any number of irrelevant factors or situations. But we were not made to question our significance, but rather, to use our innate significances to overcome the obstacles that keep

Being of Purpose

us from serving, that keep us from our purposes.

Out of all the people in the world, you…you matter for reasons you will never fully comprehend. So out of all the problems that we may have in our life spans, the last thing we should be thinking about is mattering. And quite frankly, during times when we don't genuinely think of ourselves as significant, why do we so much expect others to?

We need to get into the habit of realizing our significance apart from the obtainment of our recognition, blessings, awards, praise, accomplishments, and given miracles both big and small. Such things do not make or define us as significant but are birthed from us because we already hold such great magnificence.

In addition, when we believe in the grandness of our innate worth, our purposes don't seem nearly as clouded, invisible, or infinitesimal. When we believe that we carry greatness, our greatness will show itself to be carried. For we cannot think of ourselves as indifferent, and then wish to harness the vast power that is being, and the infinite touch of our beings that is our purpose.

Out of all the issues and situations that cause friction on our journeys, we must not let ourselves be the ones to diminish our own powers as one. We must not be fooled into believing that we fall a micron short of brilliance. We all matter, and we all are different, for this is what makes our purposes ours.

YOU ARE ALREADY DIFFERENT

ON THE JOURNEY OF JUST BEING

The best way to differentiate yourself is not merely to do things that separate you from everyone else but doing things that bring you closer to your being. Life is not so much about reinventing ourselves but more about growing into our greatest forms of being.

Falling into this notion that you should be someone other than yourself to be better or different is an incredible self-afflicting fallacy. It doesn't even make sense, for how are you going to be a better you and then deny yourself the very same premise of thought.

You don't have to be someone else to reach the success or the identity you long for. The key to reaching these things is to just be, just be more of what you already are. Again, in the name of validation, so many of us *"re-invent"* ourselves and then struggle with our identity, trying to bring and keep a being alive that cannot exist within the definition of our truest internal essence.

That is why we must understand that we are already different. No one has our fingerprints, no one has our mind. No one can authentically be you, and you can't authentically be anyone else. The only people we can be and be efficiently and effortlessly are ourselves.

With that said, there are many of those who think their identity is solely rooted in their physical existence and in the environment it inhabits. We tend to associate our identity with our social class, relationships, and our physical fitness, good, bad, or average. And though our thoughts, beliefs, and emotions may be highly correlated to such variables, because they can easily waver, they are not the core of our

Being of Purpose

identity.

Social class can escalate or decline, relationships often change as we do, and our health and physical fitness fluctuate, but the core of our identities are more so constant. That is why *"this is just who I am"* should never be confused with *"this is who I am at this moment."*

Sometimes we think that if we can be more different, our purpose will show itself to this new being even if it's not in its authentic form. But we must know that a false being will never dwell long in a place of true purpose.

Other times, when we are faced with hard times, instead of using our authentic beings to get through them, we leave behind our greatest asset in hopes that a new *"us"* will be void of such issues. We think that if we make ourselves *"different,"* then our problems won't identify with our new selves. But our problems are more stubborn than we often like them to be, which is, indeed, why they are most properly labeled as such. In actuality, it takes being to detach them, and it takes growth to erase or mitigate their presence in our lives as we cannot get past our problems without somehow passing them.

Correspondingly, we may try to change our identity during times of immense stress, as we can also suffer from the feeling and thought of our unknown, unclear, or unrefined identity being compromised or further attacked by what is going on around us. But we must realize that a seed will always grow to be the same plant of its biological makeup if it so chooses to grow. The seed does not wish or need to change into a different seed in order to persevere, all it has to do is grow. That is how it reaches greatness. That is how it takes up its shape while adding substantial meaning to the landscape around it.

> So often we confuse **GROW**th with an attack on our identity.

So often we confuse growth with an attack on our identity when really our lessons, our triumphs, and our love are all here to strengthen the recognition of who we are or who we could be when we grow into our truest forms.

The leaves of an oak still make up the oak even if the leaves are bruised. A monarch butterfly is still *Danaus plexippus* both when it is a caterpillar and also when its wings are segmented with vibrant portions of orange. You see, who we are and what we may become are nothing compared to our resilience and the part of God that lives in us that provides it.

Our identities are vastly more rooted in our growth than in the circumstances that provide such opportunities for progression. For to be is to be planted probably in the authenticity of our beings, as to be is to grow into our greatest self so that we can influence with great, bold, and enduring seeds of our own.

And as we prop ourselves up, our roots will spread more varied than others. As we heighten, our leaves unfold and our branches extend, though differently from other beings of similarity. You see, as long as we

Being of Purpose

grow, as long as we mature, our small buried or unrecognizable seeds transform into something more. Suddenly, our growth allows for our beings' identities to be larger and more easily and accurately perceived. Thus, it is unwise to search for our identities and not also search for growth, as much of the implementation of our purposes will be tied closely to our development.

Luckily for us, as our beings' contingencies are designed, our authentic self continues to just be even if we aren't growing, and often expresses the lack of personal progression by displaying, for instance, an ego or other covering of falsehood. And since it takes far more energy pretending to be than not, sometimes we don't sense our true selves again until we don't have enough energy to be anybody other than who we are meant to be. It is often here in this place that pride and egos are broken, as the reflections of our false selves are interrupted by life's true ripples.

In contrast, when we welcome who we are and the natural differences that make us whole, we easily find more of our purpose and, instead of putting so much energy into seeking our greatest beings, we can begin to use some of such energy to grow and project out our human forms of greatness onto others.

CHAPTER 10
Growing Your Greatest You

"If you are wanting to further master the journey of just being, you must also be willing to master the art of transition."

MASTERING THE ART OF TRANSITIONS

With growth or setbacks (which can create opportunities for growth) comes change, and with change, of course, comes transition. Transitions can be tricky at times, difficult to absorb and sometimes to incorporate in the destiny we have constructed for ourselves. They can seem cruel, daunting, confusing, and, without question, more difficult than the change itself. Yes, we want to move into the next phase of life, but wait…that actually requires moving, that actually requires transition. Thus, if you are wanting to further master the journey of just being, you must also be willing to master the art of transition.

In many cases, it is the transition itself that actually deters people from growing, from being more of who they could be. But the truth is that the more we grow to be, the more being becomes a part of us, the more transitions we will not only face but also boldly seek, as transitions have their purposes as well.

> **"**
> We should think of **TRANSITION**s as micro-journeys on our paths.

We should think of transitions as micro-journeys on our paths. They are the bridges, the hills, and the mud in between the water and dry land. And as such, they are incorporated in our life's work to teach us, to soothe us into our new realities, and to grow us in frequency, magnitude, and duration in the direction to that of our greater selves.

Just think if all of a sudden you woke up on the floor of an empty home with no recollection of how you got there and no memories of the past to fill the rooms and adorn the walls. Now, suddenly, moving sounds a little more entertaining. Imagine if transition bridged a way for you to leave an old relationship behind to fully find and appreciate the love you've always dreamed of, or assisted in fulfilling your greatest purposes in life. Now, such collective moments of transition seem a little worthier.

So why don't we reframe our definition of transitions so that they are not as burdensome as we often make them? In 6 diverse ways, using 6 common transitions, we can teach ourselves better perspectives when dealing with life's in-betweens.

Growing Your Greatest You

1. **Birth: Knowing your Purpose.** No matter what the struggle is, somehow when you know the purpose of your struggle, you'll find the will to push through your transition.

   One of the greatest trying transitions is birth. So much time and energy go into gestation and the actual arrival to our new homes. Our mothers carry us with back-breaking endurance. With their bladders squeezed, they eventually struggle with simple tasks such as the tying of their own shoes. For around 9 months they carried us until many of them were told to *Push! Push!*

   No, our purposes won't always be as apparent as a protruding belly. But when we know the purpose of our pain, our situations are just a little easier to tolerate, a little better to just be in.

2. **Sunrises/Sunsets: Finding the Beauty.** This can be a tricky feat, but it is often necessary to capture and fully process our highlighted silver linings. In life, we go through periods of darkness and light, but some of the most beautiful moments occur when both meet an exceptional atmospheric collision. The transition of day and night is spectacular not only to witness but also in showing us that there is often beauty in the transitioning of our being, again, even if the benefits have not yet been made apparent.

ON THE JOURNEY OF JUST BEING

3. **From the Caterpillar to the Butterfly: Dream Bigger.**
We all know that transitions can be intimidating, and they can seem big in relation to where we currently are in life. It's a good thing we were made to dream. Dreams, big dreams belittle transitions into just that of simple actions.

   And instead of focusing on all of the changes we have to go through, big dreams allow us to focus on being until we eventually come to manifest all the glory that awaits. Caterpillars feed steadfastly; they are so caught up in their dreams that it does not concern them that they cannot fly, that they don't have a mural of splendor for wings, or that they cannot drink the sweet nectar that will eventually sustain them. But they have in mind what they want to become, and so instead of losing focus, they use their actions to get them willfully to their form of aerial brilliance.

4. **From Seed to Plant: Knowing that Transitioning Means Growth.** A tree does not grow overnight, and as mentioned, we cannot properly collect a harvest without first a season of growth, without giving the objects of our beings the opportunity to just be.

Growing Your Greatest You

We must know that like a seed, our periods of growth, our transitions, are not here to make us hopeless, but rather they occur to make us fruitful.

5. **The Seasons: The Changing of Times.** Knowing that just as the seasons change things won't always be the same for our beings. And many times, there will be no need to stress, look at a watch, or create a countdown. Many times, with our stillness, all we will need to do is simply work to breathe, be, and become.

   Just as all times will not be good, all times will not be bad. But by knowing which season you are in, you will be more capable of being prepared to take in, withstand, and/or enjoy the next season.

6. **Water: Knowing You Can Make It.** Not every transition is going to seem worthwhile; deaths of loved one, layoffs and other downfalls will not portray themselves with good or logical reasons for occurring. But often, the reason for our transition is simply to show us that we can make it, to allow us to see that we are stronger than we think.

   Water is great at this. It takes on so many changes, transforms so many times and in so many ways. It flows as a liquid, flakes as snow, gases as vapor, and solidifies as ice. It covers the ground, floats away in chilly clouds, falls miles from the sky,

ON THE JOURNEY OF JUST BEING

and it still manages to survive as H_2O.

And if water can withstand so many transitions, surely, we can survive a few. After all, we are made up of about 60% of it.

So, you see, transitions aren't all that bad, and mastering them allows us to master ourselves. They provide clarity, give us the time needed to adjust, teach us, make us stronger, and show us eventually just why we should not only be but also love the practice of being. By actively working and building upon our most personal state of existence and resting within the confines of our greatest self, we can begin to choose being as our selective position of consciousness, consequently becoming great and lasting be'ers.

THE CONSCIOUS BE'ER

We'd probably like to think that at some point, perhaps, when we've reached some portion of our greatest selves, that there will be no more to learn and that all we have learned so far cannot be forgotten. But of course, our greatest selves would never find this falsehood to be true.

Even when we've reached segments of our greater selves, there is still more to learn, more to discover about our beings as we accumulate and mold our magnificence into growing a greater self in the time and

" YOU ARE your GREATest investment.

Growing Your Greatest You

circumstance it finds itself in.

Each month, find something you feel you should work on and then dive into it. You are your greatest investment, and not only will your being benefit from what should be your life's greatest practice but the world and generations to come. Loving the practice of being allows us to be just a little easier. It welcomes being and eventually transforms us graciously into conscious be'ers.

For it is one thing to practice just being and another thing to routinely or naturally just be, but a whole different thing to consciously be, as it falls into a higher realm of actively being present, as it proactively gets us to our utmost form of living.

To know as best as one can when and how to circumstantially be is how one skillfully refines their life; to know when to be still, when to let go, and when to rest when their mind finds it appropriate, or life finds it necessary. This is how we efficiently and nimbly move around life's obstacles, not only to persist but to thrive in our willingness to live far beyond the limitations of our physical existence. The conscious be'er is how one orchestrates their life so that it flows great with the purpose, spirit, and construct of one's being.

So, what is it that makes a conscious being so different from one who is just being? Well, the conscious be'er still chooses to just be, but they actively choose to be in ways more wisely decisive in any given moment or circumstance.

It is the intent, it is the ambition to want to choose, and it is the

ON THE JOURNEY OF JUST BEING

knowledge to know how to distinctively choose, that allows us to consciously be. A conscious be'er is transformed from just being to consistently just being great. They turn just being of routine into that of being a co-creator of all good things they have put to mind.

But in order to accurately and effectively use our consciousness, one must accurately use awareness, as awareness allows us insight into a situation and discernment of how to properly prepare, organize, mitigate, or remove a situation altogether.

Just being acknowledges that we are and have enough to get to the next stage in our lives. But if we lack the awareness as to why we are being, just being may appear to have little to no use or reason. This is why awareness is vital to us being great. God can send us a million and one messages in a million and one different ways (i.e. through people, good times or bad). But if we are not tuned into and aware of the message when it comes, then it's almost as if God never sent them. Then they might as well have been, at least for the moment, blank sheets of paper shredded by the winds of our problems or distractions.

> " The closer you are to something or someone the easier it is to **COMMUNICATE**.

Luckily for us, there are many ways to improve our awareness, all of which require us, of course, to just be.

1. **Find and**

Growing Your Greatest You

Continually Connect with the God in and Around You.
We all know, through friendship and family, that the closer you are to something or someone the easier it is to communicate. Take one of your closest friends for example. With just a look, you two, depending on the situation, can possibly have a whole mini conversation. In contrast, you try communicating with a stranger, and there is a good possibility you two might not even speak the same language.

Fortunately for us, God's language is universal, and though we may speak in prayer—we must also take time to listen with awareness, in moments of meditation, rest, silence, and solitude. So many of us are just talking, talking, talking but never take a moment to just be…and listen. Thankfully, God's capacity to love and speak to and within us ends at least with the boundaries we place on ourselves to hear.

For when we have a direct relationship with the sender of the message, we recognize the name and can be surer if the message belongs to us. Furthermore, when we are expecting a message to come, we can properly prepare and be on the lookout for it. Thus, too, we can more appropriately live in the moment.

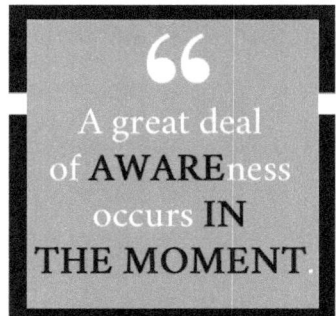

> A great deal of **AWARE**ness occurs **IN THE MOMENT**.

ON THE JOURNEY OF JUST BEING

2. **Living in the Moment.** A great deal of awareness occurs in the moment when we have the most focus, mental acuity, and the appreciation to consistently be aware. Here, in these moments, is where our lives and our beings travel parallel with one another. So often we miss these moments we're so privileged to have. Instead, our minds are set to worry, dialed into past failures, encapsulated in moments of distraction, and lost in daunting futures that may not even come to pass.

   Living in the moment allows us to better filter out all of our minds' chaos. Thus, it allows us to receive the message as it comes, creating an internal infrastructure where there are fewer losses of our shipment and much less perceived delays in delivery.

3. **Be Honest.** Being honest does not and will not ever mean that we know or should know everything about ourselves (or anyone else for that matter), but it helps us to appropriately acknowledge the things we do know.

   Honesty allows us to be aware of who we are and of all the things around us that are keeping us from being short of genuine. It keeps the internal disturbances down and also minimizes the excessive external distractions we often find in the overuse of technology and entertainment.

   Thus, it gives us time to appropriately retrieve, filter, translate, and process the many messages that are delivered.

We must begin to perceive honesty not solely as a method of constructive criticism but also as a mail room. Through imperfection, mistakes, guidance, and instinct, life will send us many messages, but it is up to us to practice being aware of the address of what is being delivered. Does this sadness really belong to me? Is this shame supposed to bear my name? Many of us have a curious habit of opening and hoarding junk mail that does not really belong to us.

Equally and unfortunately so, many of us don't open the messages legibly addressed with our name. This dream, this life, this fulfillment is addressed to me, but somehow, rather because of fear, ego, or complacency, I dare not open it.

4. **Be of Knowledge.** The term *"knowledge is power"* is more than just a cliché. Knowledge heightens both awareness and consciousness and allows us to better understand the world we live in and also the world that lives in us. It is knowledge that transforms experiential learning into that of wisdom, drawing out the light from darkness. It is knowledge that makes personal instruction easier and mitigates the fear that sometimes surrounds self-discovery.

Being aware of associated knowledge allows us to make better decisions when it comes to our intentions, as we can better

ON THE JOURNEY OF JUST BEING

lead our beings into conscious actions that serve our beings and their purposes.

And while awareness allows us to see the collection of our potential choices, consciousness is the power in the choice. For to consciously be is to choose our ways in wisdom.

Should I wallow in pity today or should I aim to heighten my esteem? Should I wait for someone or something to bring me happiness or should I use my being to create it? A conscious being moves to appropriately just be, and they trust that their authentic self will lead them most times in the best direction out of all the many ways possible.

By being conscious be'ers, we can properly maneuver our beings with skillful intent and prowess, and even greater, begin to influence positivity as we begin to move strategically the beings of those around us to betterment.

TEACHING THE POWER OF SELF

When one has touched their greatest self, they are without a doubt naturally inclined to share it with others in some aspect or another. Just as hateful people want others to hate, and the same way hurt people long to hurt people, once you've felt the bold peace of being still, you will want others to know such simple wisdom. Once you've sensed the most authentic form of happiness, you'd wish to cover the world in its quilt.

Growing Your Greatest You

And once you can just be, you'll want to teach others the same, of course, in their own individual way, as this book was consciously titled *On the Journey of Just Being,* and not *On the Journey of Just Being Another.*

For at the end of everyone's true purpose is the act of passing on their trade or ideas, and at the end of everyone's greatest self is the giving of knowledge in relation to paths of the journey made.

> " At the end of everyone's greatest self is the giving of **KNOWLEDGE** in relation to paths of the journey made.

All too often we only think to share ourselves and forget to share the ways and actions that allowed us to get to a place of being. Of course, we must keep in mind that all of us are different, and our definition of personal success may be somewhat varied from each other. But most importantly, we must realize that this is, in many ways, okay.

To expect everyone to just be like us is insane, and at best a waste of time. Innovation, creativity, and overall progression cannot stem from that form of thought. That is why we must teach those around to genuinely care and grow their own being. We must be at a certain peace (not necessarily agreeing) with other people's ideologies and decisions so long as those thoughts and actions aim to grow their being and that of others in a healthy, safe, and productive manner. Just being at our greatest capacity is not sharing our authentic self so that others can be just like us;

ON THE JOURNEY OF JUST BEING

it is about sharing our beings so that others may find the courage and will to do the same, to just be themselves.

And we share our beings not just with our words but also with our feelings, in our actions and reactions and our gestures. Happy people illicit smiles and peace clearly wears itself on people's faces. You see, we truly touch people when the good energy we carry is palpable.

And true to just being, it doesn't take much to spread the power of the self, to extend the greatness that is being to the countless, as all we have to do is just be. We must be ripples in the water, allowing the content of our greatest beings to be stretched and influenced as gentle and as tranquil as all that we embody. We must be trees in a forest, as they only have to be in their might to make the ones who view them most alive and free. We must be the sun against the horizon, coming and going in magnificence so that others may see the lighted display of what it means to endure our transitions. As a result, being in our greatest forms is less of a coax and, casually so, more of a graceful invitation to be.

Essentially, that is what our experiences in life really are—a never-ending invitation to be and be you extraordinarily—as so many good things can unfold in a single lifetime if only we allow them; if only

> **ESSENTIALLY,** that is what our experiences in life really are—a never-ending invitation to **BE**.

Growing Your Greatest You

we choose to truly become us and provide this gift to others.

THE CONCLUSION TO THE CONTINUATION OF JUST BEING

When we bloom into our greatest being, our potential becomes much more evident, our desires to reach them increase dramatically, and the excuses we often use to ignore them are blown away by the mighty winds of our movement.

Though in this encroaching world of excessive and unnecessary technology use, the glamorization of misunderstood fame, of obsessions to negative attention, egotism, and unbecoming social statuses, many of us are significantly compromising the route to ourselves. Many of us are tirelessly searching, wasting vast amounts of time and energy looking for what it means, for what it really feels like to just be. Ironically, though by the same token, we are often searching everywhere but within ourselves for the answer.

In addition to our good times, we will have to climb mountains, cross rivers, and face foes, as such is life. The potentially unfortunate thing is that if we neglect our paths' lessons, if we are unwilling to be and live in our purposes, many of our most treacherous but necessary travels will be made in vain. For when we choose to unknowingly or otherwise not be, we consequently tread exhaustively on a course to nowhere.

However, when we are comfortable being and proactively engaging in actions that lift and further our being, suddenly, courses in our lives become a little less distant and a lot less weary.

ON THE JOURNEY OF JUST BEING

Because we can physically and mentally be here at this moment, and because we are the limiting factor to just how much good we can create and pass on, the journeys to ourselves hold both the shortest paths and also offer the greatest treasures, for we are the *"X"* that marks the spot.

As we continue to just be, we must know that no matter who we are, where we live, or how we may choose to view the world, our greatest treasure is as close to us as it is ever going to be. Whether you're running on a treadmill, standing still on your commute, or sitting on a park bench taking moments to gaze away at the land, you, wherever you are, whatever you're doing or going through, have the power to change the world for the better, and all just by being true to yourself.

So, the next time you are indecisive on whether *"to be or not to be"*, hopefully, the answer will be easy. *Be*; simply, *just be*, for there is where our most worthwhile journey lies.

THE END

www.ingramcontent.com/pod-product-compliance
Lightning Source LLC
Chambersburg PA
CBHW020408080526
44584CB00014B/1236